The iPod & iTunes PocketGuide

Third Edition

Christopher **Breen**

All the Secrets of the iPod, Pocket Sized.

Peachpit Press

The iPod & iTunes Pocket Guide, Third Edition

Christopher Breen

Peachpit Press
1249 Eighth Street
Berkeley, CA 94710
510/524-2178
800/283-9444
510/524-2221 (fax)

Find us on the Web at: www.peachpit.com
To report errors, please send a note to errata@peachpit.com

Peachpit Press is a division of Pearson Education

Managing editor: Clifford Colby
Editor: Kathy Simpson
Production editor: Simmy Cover
Compositor & Illustrator: WolfsonDesign
Indexer: Rebecca Plunkett
Cover design: Aren Howell
Cover photography: Damon Hampson
Interior design: Kim Scott, with Maureen Forys

ISBN-13: 978-0-321-52462-1
ISBN-10: 0-321-52462-4

9 8 7 6 5 4 3

Printed and bound in the United States of America

Dedication

One more time, with feeling:
To my little iBreen, Addie.

Acknowledgments

This book would be just another unrealized intriguing idea if not for the dedication of the following individuals.

At Peachpit Press: Cliff Colby, who, with armor donned and sword unsheathed, prevailed in the epic Battle for More Pages; Kathy Simpson, who wore the many hats of editor/copy editor/proofreader in such a jaunty and accomplished manner; and production pro Simmy Cover, who so capably fed raw copy into one end of the machine and extracted oh-so-pretty pages from the other. Thanks also to WolfsonDesign for creating such beautiful iPod screens and to master indexer Rebecca Plunkett for making it possible for you to easily find the book's more arcane bits of information.

At home: My wife, Claire, who never once sputtered, "What? *Another* book? You just finished one!" but instead carried on, holding the house together. And my daughter, Addie, who gave her Dada a huge smile and welcome hug at the end of every working day.

Abroad: The *Macworld* crew, who keep me in iPods. Teresa Brewer and Stan Ng at Apple for answering some of my questions. And the boys from System 9 for their continued cool-cattedness.

And, of course, Apple's iPod and iTunes teams. Get some sleep; you deserve it!

Contents

Getting Started

Though I admire your desire to learn more about your iPod by purchasing this little guide, my guess is that before you delve too deeply into this book, you'd like to actually use your iPod. That's what this chapter is for—getting you up and running as quickly as possible. Here are the steps to take:

1. Open the box.

   After you've ripped the wrapping off your iPod, try turning it on. If it recently came from the factory, it could be charged and nearly ready to play.

   To switch on any display-bearing iPod except the iPod touch, press and hold any of the iPod's buttons. (I have the best luck pressing the Center button in the middle of the click wheel.) If the iPod is charged, it should display the Apple logo after a few seconds and then be ready to roll in about 30 seconds. If nothing happens when you try to start the iPod, make sure that the Hold switch isn't on. (The iPod classic's Hold switch is on the top, and the latest iPod nano's Hold switch is on the bottom.) If you see any orange next to the switch, that means the Hold switch is on. Slide the switch over to disengage it. If the iPod still won't start, it must be charged.

To switch on the iPod touch, briefly press its Sleep/Wake button (the single button on the top). If the touch has any power in it, the Apple logo appears on the screen; then the touch's interface appears beneath its crisp glass display.

For the iPod shuffle, push the power switch to the right. If a light shows on the LED next to the switch (green or amber), the iPod is charged enough for you to play with it. If no light shows, it needs charging.

2. Charge it (if necessary).

If the iPod doesn't work out of the box, you need to charge it up. On an iPod with a display (any iPod except the iPod shuffle), you can do this by plugging the included USB cable into your computer's powered USB 2.0 port and plugging the other end of the cable into the bottom of the iPod. If you have a charger for your iPod (chargers are optional for all iPods), you can plug the cable's

USB connector into the charger instead of your computer, plug the other end of the cable into your iPod, and plug the charger into a wall socket.

The iPod shuffle is charged from your computer's powered USB port via its included USB Dock. Plug the Dock into a powered USB port to charge the iPod.

3. Install iTunes.

If you don't already have a current copy of iTunes on your computer, download it from www.apple.com/itunes/download. (Apple no longer bundles a CD copy of iTunes with the iPod.) Follow whatever onscreen directions are necessary to put iTunes on your Windows PC or Mac.

4. Rip a CD.

No, don't actually rip the disc in half. *Rip* in this context mean to transfer the audio from the CD to your computer. To do this, insert the disc into your computer's CD or DVD drive, and launch iTunes (if it doesn't launch automatically after you've inserted the disc). By default, iTunes 7 and later tosses up a dialog box that reads "Would you like to import the CD *nameofCD* into your iTunes library?" (where *nameofCD* is the name of your CD). Click Yes, and iTunes will convert the audio files to a format that can be played on the iPod. Also, the tracks you ripped from the CD will appear in iTunes' main window when you click the Music entry in the iTunes Source list.

To import that CD at a later time, click No in this dialog box. Then, later, select the CD in the Source list, and click the Import CD button in the bottom-right corner of the iTunes window.

5. Plug in the iPod.

If it's not plugged in already, plug your iPod into your computer. For an iPod other than an iPod shuffle, this means stringing the included USB cable between a powered USB 2.0 port on the computer and the Dock Connector port on the bottom of the iPod. If you have a display-bearing iPod other than a nano, fifth-generation (5G) iPod, iPod classic, or iPod touch, you can use an optional FireWire cable instead of the USB cable.

The second- and third-generation (2G and 3G) iPod shuffles require the Dock that comes with them; just plug the Dock's cable into a free USB 2.0 port. Original iPod shuffle models (the ones that look like a fat stick of gum) have a built-in USB connector that plugs directly into your computer.

After you plug in your iPod for the first time, a window will pop up, asking you to name your iPod. Feel free to accept or ignore Apple's invitation to register your iPod at this point.

If your computer is connected to the Internet, the iTunes Store window will open within the main iTunes window. Yes, Apple wants you to shop, but you don't have to.

If you have any music in your iTunes Library, iTunes will ask you whether you'd like to import album artwork for your display-bearing iPod.

Unless you have a dial-up connection to the Internet, let iTunes retrieve this artwork; it will make using your iPod and iTunes a more enjoyable experience (as you'll read later). If you have lots of tracks in your library—more than a few thousand—retrieving that artwork can take a while.

iTunes will also seek out tracks that should be played gaplessly—such as music from albums like Pink Floyd's *Dark Side of the Moon* or any number of classical recordings in which one track should flow seamlessly into another.

Although iTunes 7 and later can play music gaplessly, this feature is supported only on 5G and later full-size iPods (including the iPod touch and iPhone) and on 2G and 3G iPod nanos. All earlier iPods play music with short gaps between tracks.

6. Transfer music to the iPod.

By default, the iPod is configured so that it updates its music library automatically when it's connected to your computer. The music you ripped from your CD should transfer to the iPod quickly. If it doesn't, simply choose File > Sync *Name of Your iPod* (where *Name of Your iPod* is... well, the name of your iPod).

7. Unmount and play.

When the music has finished transferring, locate the name of your iPod in iTunes' Source list, and click the little Eject icon next to it. When the iPod disappears from iTunes, unplug it from your computer.

Unwrap the earbuds that came with the iPod, jam them into your ears, and plug the other end into the iPod's Headphone port. On an iPod with a click wheel, rotate your thumb around the wheel on the front until Shuffle Songs is selected and then press the iPod's Center button. On an iPod touch, press the Home button (the single round button on the face of the iPod), slide the arrow slider to the right to unlock the iPod, tap the Music icon at the bottom of the display, tap a playlist in the resulting Playlist screen, and tap Shuffle. On an iPod shuffle, just switch the iPod on by sliding the power switch to the On position and then pressing the Play button on the front of the shuffle.

To adjust the volume on a click-wheel iPod, rotate your thumb clockwise to increase volume and counterclockwise to turn it down. On an iPod touch, drag the volume slider in the Now Playing screen. On a shuffle, press the plus (+) symbol on the top of the control ring to crank it up and the minus (–) symbol below to make it quieter.

8. Enjoy.

1

Meet the iPod

My guess is that you wouldn't be reading these words if an iPod weren't already part of your life—or weren't soon to be part of your life. Congratulations. You've chosen to ally yourself with the world's most popular and—in my humble opinion—finest portable music player.

Oh, sure, there have been pretenders to the throne, countless "iPod killers" that on closer examination proved to be nothing more than less-capable and less-stylish wannabes. Despite multiple attempts to diminish its dominance, the iPod remains It—*the* music player to own.

And now that you do, it's time to become better acquainted with your multimedia buddy. To get started, let's tour the various iPod models and rummage around in the iPod's box.

Today's iPods

The danger of slapping a heading like "Today's iPods" in a book like this one is that—given Apple's habit of revving the iPod line every 6 to 9 months—Today's iPods may be Yesterday's iPods by the time you read this chapter. Unless the next-generation iPods breathe fire and project high-definition movies, however, the iPod you own shouldn't be disturbingly different from what I'm writing about in the autumn of 2007. Here's the lineup.

iPod touch

In the early summer of 2007, Apple released a little something called the iPhone. Maybe you've heard of it. With the iPhone came the promise of an iPod that could be controlled not by a wheel or series of buttons, but the touch of a finger. A few months later, the iPod touch delivered on that promise (**FIGURE 1.1**). Like the iPhone, it bears a touchscreen display that you control by tapping, flicking, pinching, and dragging objects on its screen. (See the sidebar "iPod touch's Full Gestures" for more information on controlling your touch.)

Figure 1.1
iPod touch.

Photo courtesy of Apple, Inc.

iPod touch's Full Gestures

The iPod touch's screen is deliberately . . . well, *touchy,* because touching it is how you control the device. These are the gestures you'll use to navigate and control your iPod touch.

Tap

You're going to see the word *tap* a lot in this book when I discuss the iPod touch. When you want to initiate an action—launch an application, control the iPod's playback features, flip an object around, or move to the next screen—you'll likely use this gesture.

continues on next page

iPod touch's Full Gestures *continued*

DOUBLE TAP

Sometimes, just one tap won't do. Double-tapping often enlarges or contracts an image—zooms in on a photo or Web page, for example, or returns it to its normal size after you've enlarged it. At other times, double-tapping makes items return to the previous view. Double-tap a playlist in Cover Flow view, for example, to flip the playlist back to the album artwork.

FLICK

If you want to scroll up or down a long playlist rapidly, zip through a selection of album covers in the iPod's Cover Flow view (a view that allows you to browse your music and podcast collection by album cover/artwork), or flip from one photo to another, you use the flick gesture. The faster you flick, the faster the iPod attempts to match your action by scrolling or zipping more rapidly. Slower flicks produce less motion on the display. To stop the motion initiated by a flick, just place your finger on the display. Motion stops instantly.

DRAG

For finer control, drag your finger across the display. Use this motion to scroll down a list in a controlled way or to reposition an enlarged image or Web page. You also drag the iPod volume slider and playhead when you're playing music or videos.

STRETCH/PINCH

To expand an image—a photo or Web page—place your thumb and index finger together on the iPhone's display and then stretch them apart. To make an image smaller, start with your thumb and finger apart; then pinch them together.

TOUCH AND DRAG

This gesture isn't terribly common but is helpful nonetheless. To edit text, touch the display until a magnifier appears. Drag to where you'd like to insert new text (a cursor marks the spot); then let go. In the Music area's More screen, you'll find the option to swap out icons along the bottom of the display by touching and dragging new icons into place. You also touch and drag entries in the On-The-Go playlist to change their positions in the list.

The iPod touch is sort of a hybrid between a regular iPod and the iPhone. As I mention earlier in this section, it has a display and interface similar to the iPhone's. It also includes wireless networking circuitry (Wi-Fi). It has the same media capabilities as the iPhone, letting you play music and videos, view slideshows, and watch YouTube videos streamed across the Web. And just as you can with an iPhone, you can purchase music directly on the touch via the iTunes Wi-Fi Music Store (and, eventually, from participating Starbucks outlets).

The touch also includes the Calendar, Clock, Contacts, and Calculator applications, as well as the Safari Web browser. Currently, though, it doesn't offer an email client or such Internet-friendly iPhone applications as Stocks, Maps, and Weather. And of course, you can't make a call with an iPod touch.

As this book goes to press, the iPod touch comes in capacities of 8 GB and 16 GB, priced at $299 and $399, respectively. Apple claims that the 8 GB touch will hold up to 1,750 4-minute songs encoded in AAC format at 128 Kbps. (I explain all this encoding stuff in Chapter 4.) The 16 GB model can hold up to 3,500 audio tracks encoded the same way. A 2-hour movie purchased from the iTunes Store consumes around 1.3 GB, and an hour-long TV show (really, around 43 minutes when the commercials have been stripped out) eats up close to 500 MB. Given the girth of these videos, it's clear that you're not going to pack the entire *Pink Panther* oeuvre plus four seasons of "Lost" onto your iPod touch.

Like all iPods, this model is powered by a recharge-able lithium-ion battery. Constant play time between charges on iPods varies depending on the model you own. Among the various iPod models, the iPod touch offers the least continuous play time. Apple suggests that these iPods can play music continuously for up to 22 hours, but your mileage will vary depending on whether you have Wi-Fi switched on or off. (Wi-Fi consumes a fair amount of battery power even when it's supposedly doing nothing.)

iPod touch: Entering and Editing Text

The various taps, pinches, and drags will get you where you want to go, but they won't create a contact for you or help you correct spelling mistakes when you're filling in a Web site's form. The iPod touch's keyboard and a well-placed finger will do these jobs.

TOUCH TYPING

This iPod's virtual keyboard largely matches the configuration of your computer's keyboard. You'll find an alphabetic layout when you open most applications. To capitalize characters, tap the up-arrow key (the iPod's Shift key). To view numbers and most punctuation, tap the .?123 key. To see less-used characters (including £, ¥, and €), choose the numbers layout by tapping the .?123 key and then tapping the #+= key. The Space, Return, and Delete keys do exactly what you'd expect.

To make typing easier, the keyboard's layout changes depending on the application you're using. In Safari, for example, the default layout shows period (.), slash (/), and .com keys along the bottom. And unlike any other iPod application, Safari lets you display a keyboard in Landscape view, which gives you more room to type.

 When you type a character, its magnified image appears as you touch it. If you tap the wrong character, leave your finger where it is, and slide it to the character you want; the character won't be "typed" until you let go.

continues on next page

iPod touch: Entering and Editing Text *continued*

EDITING TEXT

The iPod touch offers a unique way to edit text. You needn't tap the Delete key time and again to work your way back to your mistake; instead, tap and hold the line of text you want to edit. When you do, a magnifying glass appears, showing a close-up view of the area under your finger. Inside this magnified view is a blinking cursor. Drag the cursor to where you want to make your correction—after the word or letter you want to correct—and then use the Delete key to remove the text. In most cases, you can also tap between words to insert the cursor there.

iPod classic

To keep the various iPod models straight in the past, I've referred to the many full-size iPod models by their generation. The original iPod was the first-generation (or 1G) iPod. The last full-size iPod, released before the autumn of 2007, was the 5G iPod. Although I'll continue to refer to some current iPod models by their generation—specifically, the current-as-we-go-to-press 3G iPod shuffle and the 3G iPod nano—I can skip this generational jargon for today's full-size, click-wheel iPod. Due in large part to the existence of the wholly new iPod touch, Apple has given the former "full-size" iPod a new designation: the iPod classic (**FIGURE 1.2**).

Figure 1.2

iPod classic.

Photo courtesy
of Apple, Inc.

Currently available in a $249 80 GB silver or black
case (with traditional shiny chrome back) or a similarly hued $349 160 GB configuration, these iPods
are all about storage. The 80 GB model will hold up
to 20,000 4-minute songs, and as simple arithmetic
tells us, the 160 GB version holds 40,000 4-minute
128 Kbps AAC songs (or just over 111 days of continuous music). As for video, the 160 GB iPod classic will
hold up to 200 hours of video encoded with Apple's
H.264 video encoder at a resolution of 640 by 480.
(Again, I provide the ins and outs of video encoding
elsewhere in the book.) And although the classic's
hard drive could hold more, these iPods are limited
to storing *just* 25,000 photos. Both classics sport
a bright 2.5-inch (measured diagonally) display and
offer a colorful new interface, featuring album artwork
in the first couple of layers of that interface.

Like all iPods, this model is powered by a recharge-
able lithium-ion battery. Constant play time between
charges on these iPods varies, depending on the
model you own. The 80 GB iPod plays music for
around 36 hours or video for around 6 hours on a
single charge if you refrain from mucking too much
with the iPod's controls, switch off EQ and Sound
Check, and leave backlighting off. The 160 GB iPod
can play music continuously for more than 50 hours
and video for approximately 10 hours. Apple suggests
that the lower-capacity classic will play video to a
connected TV set for up to 5 hours on a single battery
charge, whereas the 160 GB classic will play for up to
7 hours on its charge. (In Chapter 8, I tell you how to
get the greatest life out of that battery charge.)

iPod nano (3G)

The 3G iPod nano (**Figure 1.3**) can be silver, blue,
green, black, or red. It's colorful on the inside as well;
just like the iPod classic, it can show pictures and
slideshows, colorful album art, and video. Like the
iPod classic, the sleek nano bears a crisp, colorful
display (2 inches measured diagonally, rather than
2.5 inches) and sports a click-wheel control. Like its
larger siblings, it has a Dock connector on the bottom;
unlike those larger iPods, it has the Headphone port
and Hold switch on the bottom too.

Figure 1.3
iPod nano.

Photo courtesy
of Apple, Inc.

Apple offers the nano in two configurations: the
$149 4 GB iPod nano, which comes only in silver; and
the $199 8 GB iPod nano, available in silver, green,
blue, black, and a color Apple calls (PRODUCT) RED.
(A portion of the price of the red nano goes to the
Global Fund to fight AIDS in Africa.) The 4 GB model
holds approximately 1,000 songs, and the 8 GB nano
can pack in up to 2,000 songs. The lower-capacity
nano can hold up to 3,500 pictures, whereas the 8 GB
nano can carry up to 7,000 photos.

Unlike the larger iPods, the iPod nano has no internal
moving parts. Instead of a hard drive, it uses flash-
media chips—solid-state storage circuitry—to store
music and data. In addition to being tiny, these chips
offer a singular advantage: They make playback
skip-proof. Playback on a full-size iPod can skip if
you're playing long or large tracks, or if you bounce
around a lot, as you might while exercising. This
issue doesn't come up with the nano, as music is
fed immediately from the flash chip to the nano's

amplifier. This arrangement makes the nano an ideal workout companion. (The iPod shuffle, which is the subject of the next section, also uses flash media.)

Battery life on the nano is quite good. Apple claims approximately 24 hours of music play time, but I've managed to make my 8 GB nano play music for nearly 30 hours. Apple's suggestion that the nano will play video for around 5 hours is accurate. Like the 80 GB classic, the nano will play for around 5 hours on one battery charge when you project video from your nano to a connected TV.

iPod shuffle (3G)

The 3G iPod shuffle is exactly the same as the 2G shuffle except that it comes in some new hues—muted shades of green, blue, and purple, as well as silver and PRODUCT (RED). The shuffle is Apple's displayless iPod, one that's about the size of a matchbox and that includes no screen to indicate what it's playing. Unlike the other iPods, the iPod shuffle (**FIGURE 1.4**) has no Dock Connector port. Instead, it sports a Headphone jack that also acts as a data syncing and power port. To sync and charge the shuffle, plug it into the included USB Dock and then plug that Dock into your computer's USB port.

Figure 1.4
iPod shuffle.

Photo courtesy
of Apple, Inc.

Although the shuffle has a controller in the shape of a wheel, the wheel doesn't spin; you simply press the wheel's outer ring to adjust volume and move from track to track (or to fast-forward or rewind through the currently playing track), and use the wheel's Center button to play or pause the shuffle.

The iPod shuffle can be had in a single $79 1 GB configuration, which holds approximately 240 songs. As I mention earlier in this chapter, the shuffle uses flash memory rather than a hard drive, which makes it another good choice for the gym.

This iPod also has a lithium-ion battery (though it's very, very small). Apple rates constant play time between charges at around 12 hours for the shuffle.

Given the shuffle's price and size, you can understand that it has certain limitations. The lack of a display is the most obvious one. This iPod is not the one to own if you want to find and play a specific track easily. Instead, you should think of the iPod shuffle as your personal radio station—one that you've programmed with your favorite music so that you won't care which song it plays.

Because it lacks a display, the shuffle doesn't hold pictures, contacts, or calendars, which other iPod models can display. It can't record audio from an outside source, either. Also, it won't play tracks encoded in certain formats. It can play AAC, AIFF, MP3, and WAV files, but not Apple Lossless files. (I discuss encoders and formats when I visit iTunes in Chapter 4.) The shuffle is exactly what it appears to be: a basic music player.

Thinking Inside the Box

At one time, Apple stuffed the iPod box with loads of goodies: in-ear headphones, a couple of cables for transferring data between your computer and iPod, a power adapter, a Dock and case for more-expensive iPods, a belt clip (for the iPod mini), a video cable for iPods with color screens, a software CD and documentation, and (of course) the iPod itself. Rummage around in the box of an iPod you've purchased in the past couple of months, and you'll find that many of these items are missing, available now only as $29 to $49 add-ons.

No worries—what is in the box provides you enough to get started. Here's what you'll find inside the various iPod boxes.

Earbuds

Your iPod comes with a set of headphones that you place inside—rather than over—your ears. Headphones of this style are known as *earbuds*. A pair of foam earbud covers accompanied earlier iPods; Apple now offers a new earbud design that lacks these disks.

Just as you'll find a wide range of foot and head sizes among groups of people, the size of the opening to the ear varies. The earbuds included with 1G iPods were a little larger than other earbuds you may have seen. Some people (including your humble author) found these headphones uncomfortable. Later iPods included smaller earbuds that I found much more comfortable. I find that without the foam disks, the latest headphones don't fit my ears terribly well; they just won't stay in a position where I can hear the audio "sweet spot." If, like me, you find the earbuds unsatisfactory, you can purchase smaller or larger earbuds, or you can opt for a pair of over-the-ear headphones.

If the included earbuds do fit you, you may or may not be pleased with their performance. Apple made great efforts to create the finest music player on the planet, and it didn't skimp on the headphones, but sound is subjective, and you may find that other headphones deliver a more pleasing sound to your ears. If you believe you deserve better sound than your Apple earbuds provide, by all means audition other headphones.

USB 2.0 cable

The iPod's proprietary Dock connector (that thin port on the bottom of the iPod) is the avenue for transferring both music and information on and off the iPod and for charging the device. Likewise, the USB 2.0 cable included with the iPod can perform double duty. When you string the cable between your iPod and your computer's powered USB 2.0 port, power flows through the cable and charges the iPod's battery. At the same time, this connection allows you to swap data—in the form of music and other files—between the player and the computer.

note The USB cable also can be attached to Apple's optional $29 iPod USB Power Adapter to charge the iPod's battery when it's not connected to a computer.

As the iPod shuffle already comes with a Dock, a USB cable is unnecessary, as is the following item.

iPod Dock Adapter

This adapter looks similar to the Dock cradle adapters included with some iPod accessories. To assist iPod accessory manufacturers, which were forced to come up with a new cradle design every time Apple issued a new iPod, Apple created a single one-size-fits-all-with-the-right-Apple-adapter specification for companies that participate in the Made for iPod program. This is that adapter. Currently, many accessories—including speakers and Docks—support this universal adapter.

Dock (iPod shuffle only)

As I mention earlier in the chapter, you power and sync the 3G iPod shuffle through a USB Dock bundled in the box. This Dock bears a single male Headphone jack. Connect the USB side of the cable to a powered USB port to charge and sync the iPod; then jack it into an Apple Power Adapter to charge the iPod.

Stand (iPod touch only)

That hunk of plastic you find inside the iPod touch's box is not an errant piece of packaging; it's a stand for holding up the iPod so you can view pictures and photos more comfortably.

Polishing cloth (iPod touch only)

As you can imagine, any device you control by smearing your finger across its face is going to get smudgy. This soft black cloth is included for wiping those smudges away.

Guides and documentation

It seems that you can't buy something as simple as a toaster these days without also gaining mounds of accompanying documentation. Apple is different in this regard. The current iPods come with a slim Quick Start guide and a product-information pamphlet that carries the fine print.

Given that you own this book, you can skip nearly all the paperwork that comes with your iPod (unless the fine print of licensing agreements helps you sleep at night). At one time, I would have sent you to the bundled CD to gawk at Apple's iPod manual or to install iTunes, but Apple has dispensed with the CD, figuring that you can obtain iTunes and any technical information from its Web site.

Yesterday's iPods

I'd like to think that a lot of old iPods are being passed from person to person as the original owners trade up. It's quite possible that you have an older iPod yet are new to this whole iPod business. This section is for you. Here's how the various models shake out.

First-generation (1G) iPod

As the name implies, these models are the very first iPods. Released in late 2001 and early 2002, the 1G iPod is offered in 5 GB and 10 GB configurations, and it bears a mechanical scroll wheel—a wheel, unlike the one on later iPods, that actually turns. Nothing on the back of an original 5 GB iPod indicates its storage capacity; the 10 GB model is marked as such on the back plate. These iPods support FireWire connections only and are incompatible with today's Dock-connector accessories. They also don't play files in the Apple Lossless format or record audio from an external source. Like all iPods up to the current full-size iPod, this iPod is incapable of playing video files.

Second-generation (2G) iPod

The second white iPod comes in 5, 10, and 20 GB capacities; sports a touch-sensitive scroll wheel; includes redesigned earbuds that fit smaller ear canals more comfortably; and slaps a plastic cover over the FireWire port. This iPod bears the same limitations as the 1G iPod in terms of support for Apple Lossless, Dock-connector accessories, audio recording, and video playback.

Third-generation (3G) iPod

Whereas the 2G iPods were an evolutionary release, the 3G players are a redefinition of the original. These iPods—available in capacities of 10, 15, 20, 30, and 40 GB —are sleeker and lighter. They feature an updated front-panel design that places touch-sensitive (and

backlit) navigation buttons above the scroll wheel.
Gone is the FireWire connector at the top of the iPod,
replaced by a proprietary connector at the bottom
of the unit that supports both FireWire and USB 2.0
connections. (Charging over USB is not supported
on these iPods, however.) An updated remote
connector is also added to the top of the 3G iPod.
This connector is ostensibly for connecting the Apple
iPod Remote to the player, but it's also used by other
accessories, such as Griffin Technology's iTrip FM
transmitter and Belkin's Voice Recorder for iPod.

iPod mini (1G and 2G)

In January 2004, Apple released a smaller version
of the iPod: the iPod mini. The 1G minis are available
in five colors: gold, silver, blue, green, and pink. The
original mini is the first iPod to hold a 4 GB hard
drive (called a *microdrive*), as well as the first iPod to
sport a click wheel. The 2G minis come in brighter
shades of blue, green, and pink (gold was discontinued after 1G, and the silver model looks the same
as the 1G version), and is offered in 4 GB and 6 GB
configurations. The mini was discontinued with the
introduction of the iPod nano.

Fourth-generation (4G) iPod

When Apple announced the 4G iPod in July 2004,
it could have done so by proclaiming that the
"maxi-mini" was born, for in some ways, the 4G iPod
is closer in design to the iPod mini than to the previous three generations of white iPods. Available in
20 GB and 40 GB configurations, the 4G iPod bears

the same kind of click-wheel controller used on the mini, and like the mini, it can be charged via USB 2.0.

Apple iPod + HP, Apple iPod mini + HP, Apple iPod shuffle + HP

At one time, Hewlett-Packard sold iPods. No longer. These iPods are unique because . . . well, because they were sold by HP. Other than that, they're functionally identical to Apple's iPods. The only real difference between an hPod and an iPod is the warranty. HP's warranty was a bit more generous in terms of when you'd have to begin paying to have your iPod fixed. HP canceled its iPod partnership with Apple in the summer of 2005.

iPod U2 Special Edition (monochrome version)

Though functionally identical to a 20 GB mono-chrome 4G iPod, this special player is the first "big" iPod to come in colors—specifically, a black face with a red click wheel. This special iPod also carries the signatures of the four U2 members etched on the back plate.

iPod photo

You can think of the iPod photo as being either a 4G iPod with color and photo capabilities or as the succeeding color-display iPod with *photo* appended to its name. This iPod—available in capacities of 30, 40, and 60 GB—is the higher-priced alternative to the monochrome 4G iPod. In addition to putting a bright and colorful face on the now-dull-in-comparison 4G iPod, the iPod photo allows you to view pictures and slideshows on your iPod (up to 25,000 pictures on the 60 GB model), as well as to project those pictures on an attached television or compatible projector.

iPod with color display

Apple did little more than make this iPod's name more cumbersome to differentiate it from the earlier iPod photo; it sports no change worthy of terming it the 5G iPod. Beginning with this model, all full-size iPods offer color. The iPod with color display comes in 20, 30, and 60 GB configurations.

iPod shuffle (1G)

The original iPod shuffle is about the size of a pack of gum and can be had in capacities of 512 MB and 1 GB. Unlike the current shuffle, this one bears a male USB connector, which allows you to jack the iPod into your computer's USB port without the need for a Dock.

iPod nano (1G)

This model is the original iPod nano. Its face is easily scratched plastic, and its back is shiny silver, like the backs of full-size iPods. It comes in capacities of 1, 2, and 4 GB and in just two colors (black and white), and it doesn't support voice memos.

Fifth-generation (5G) iPod

This iPod is the original iPod with video. It differs from the late-2006 model in that its screen isn't as bright, and it doesn't offer that model's alphabetic search feature (more on this in Chapter 3).

Fifth-generation (5G) iPod (late 2006)

Some wags refer to this model as the 5.5G iPod. As I just stated, it has a brighter screen than the original 5G iPod, as well as a search feature that's missing from the original 5G.

iPod nano (2G)

The second-generation nano has the same longish body as the original nano, but it sports a full metal jacket, reminiscent of the iPod mini. It comes in silver, blue, green, pink, (PRODUCT) RED, and black, and in capacities of 2, 4, and 8 GB. Unlike today's somewhat squattier nano, it has a 1.5-inch color screen and doesn't play video.

Phoning It In

When is an iPod not an iPod (and, therefore, worthy of nothing more than this small sidebar)? When it's a phone (and no, I don't mean *that* phone). Motorola was the first to release an iTunes-compatible mobile phone: the ill-fated ROKR. Why ill-fated? It was a little clunky-looking; it took forever to sync music because of its USB 1.1 interface; and it held a scant 100 tracks. Motorola later released the SLVR, a sleeker phone, but it suffers the same 100-track limit and slow USB 1.1 data-transfer rate.

2

Touching the
iPod touch

The iPod touch and the "traditional" iPod nano and classic are completely different beasts with regard to controls and interface. As such, they merit their own chapters. I'll begin with the most tactile member of the family: the iPod touch.

Physical Controls and Ports

The controls on the iPod touch couldn't be more minimal (**FIGURE 2.1**). Search all you like, but you won't find a click wheel, Center button, or volume switch. The iPod touch has exactly two buttons. At the bottom of the iPod's display, you'll find a single indented round button. This is the Home button, and as its name implies, it takes you to the touch's Home screen nearly every time you press it. (OK, I'll end the suspense. You also use the Home button to wake up your sleeping iPod. When you do, you don't go home; rather, you view the last screen that was visible when the iPod took a nap.)

Figure 2.1
The iPod touch.

Photo courtesy of
Apple, Inc.

Sleep/Wake switch

Home button

Headphone port
Dock Connector port

On the top-left edge of the iPod touch is a tiny black switch, which Apple describes as the Sleep/Wake button. It also switches the iPod on and off. To lock the iPod, press this button. (To unlock the iPod, press the Home button.) To switch the iPod off, press and hold the Sleep/Wake button for a few seconds until you see a red slider onscreen, labeled Slide to Power Off. Drag the slider to the right to switch off the touch (or tap Cancel to belay that order).

Smack-dab in the middle of the iPod's bottom edge is the familiar-to-iPod-owners Dock Connector port. This port is a proprietary 30-pin connector used for syncing the iPod and attaching such accessories as power adapters, FM transmitters, and speaker systems. Next to the Dock Connector port is the Headphone jack, which accommodates the iPod's white headset plug. Unlike on the iPhone, this port is not recessed, so you can use it with any set of head-phones that has a miniplug connector (the 3.5mm connector used on modern headphones).

The Touchscreen

The iPod touch earns its name from its touchscreen interface. Chapter 1 describes how you manipulate that touchscreen with taps, flicks, drags, and pinches. This section examines what you're likely to find under your fingers.

Home screen

Like the iPhone, the iPod touch has a Home screen that acts as the gateway to the iPod's many functions. The screen is laid out this way.

Status bar

The very top of the iPod's Home screen can display the following items:

iPod name. Yes, the word *iPod* is displayed in the status bar, in case you might mistake the touch for a candy bar (or, more likely, for your iPhone).

 Wi-Fi status icon. This icon indicates that the iPod is connected to a Wi-Fi network. The more bars you see, the stronger the signal.

 Lock icon. This icon appears if the iPod is locked.

 Play icon. If your iPod is playing, this icon appears.

 Alarm icon. If you've set an alarm within the iPod's Clock application, the alarm icon appears.

 Battery icon. The battery icon is always present to indicate one of a few states. If the iPod is unplugged, the battery will be some shade of green or red. Fully green means that the iPod is fully (or nearly fully) charged. The less green you see, the less power the iPod has. If you see red in the battery icon, you've got little power left.

The battery icon shows one of two symbols within the battery when the iPod is plugged into a powered USB port or power adapter. A lightning bolt tells you that the battery is charging. A picture of a plug indicates that the iPod is fully charged.

Media icons

Along the bottom of the display, you'll find the Media icons:

 Music. As the name implies, you tap this icon, and the music portion of the iPod—complete with playlists, albums, artists, and songs—appears.

 Videos. When you're ready to watch a movie, TV show, music video, or video podcast, this icon is the one to tap.

 Photos. The photos synced to your iPod via iTunes (and yes, you'll get well into syncing your iPod in Chapter 4) appear when you tap the Photos icon.

 iTunes. In addition to having the slickest interface of any iPod, the iPod touch has a unique talent: You can use it to purchase and download music from the iTunes Store. This iTunes icon is the iPod touch's gateway to a special wireless version of The Store called the iTunes Wi-Fi Music Store (which I cover in Chapter 5).

Applications and Settings

The iPod touch lets you do more than just play and purchase media. In the top portion of the Home screen, you'll find the touch's application icons and the Settings icon. They shake out this way:

 Safari. The iPod touch, being a wireless networking device, includes a fully functioning Web browser— a *real* Web browser, unlike the limited, rinky-dink browsers you find in smart phones other than Apple's iPhone. For more information on Safari, turn to Chapter 6.

 YouTube. Thanks again to the iPod touch's wireless networking capabilities, you can stream video content to your iPod touch from the popular YouTube video-sharing site. Again, see Chapter 6.

 Calendar. The iPod touch has a calendar, too. Unlike the iPhone, the touch doesn't let you enter calendar events directly, but you can sync calendars that you create on your computer to this application. You find more information on the Calendar application, as well as calendars on other iPod models, in Chapter 7.

 Contacts. Although the iPod touch is hardly a full-blown personal information manager (PIM), it does sport a mighty nice contact manager—one that you can use not only to sync contacts from your computer, but also to create contacts directly on the iPod. Chapter 7 covers contacts.

 Clock. The iPod touch can tell time (both where you live and in other parts of the world). The Clock application also includes alarm, stopwatch, and timer functions.

Calculator. Never be embarrassed by accidentally stiffing your server again. Just discreetly pull out your iPod touch and calculate a generous tip with this application. I take a look at Calculator later in this chapter.

 Settings. Tap the Settings icon, and you find a screen for adjusting the...well, *settings* of the iPod's various functions. I also discuss Settings later in the chapter.

Cover Flow

Tap the Music icon near the bottom-left corner of your iPod's screen, wait for the Playlists screen to appear (which it does by default when you first tap Music), and immediately turn the iPod on its side. You're witnessing the iPod's Cover Flow feature, a view that lets you browse your music collection and podcasts by their album or program artwork (**FIGURE 2.2**). I don't care if you never choose to browse your music this way—this iPod feature is the one you'll choose first to impress your friends. They can't help but ooh in awe when you flick your finger across the screen and the artwork flips by.

Figure 2.2
Cover Flow view.

Should you want to listen to your music or podcasts
with Cover Flow view on, you'll find that easy to do:

1. Turn the iPod to a landscape orientation (it
   doesn't matter which direction you turn; it works
   either way), and wipe your finger across the
   display to move through your audio collection.

   Albums are sorted by the artist's first name,
   so *Al Green* appears near the beginning, and
   The Yardbirds appears close to the end.

2. When you find an album you want to listen to,
   tap its cover.

   The artwork flips around and reveals a track
   list of the album's contents or, in the case of a
   podcast, the podcast episodes (**Figure 2.3**). As
   with other lists on the iPod that may be longer
   than the screen, you're welcome to flick your
   finger up the display to move down through
   the list.

Figure 2.3
A track list in
Cover Flow view.

3. Tap the track you want to listen to.

Playback begins from that track and plays to the end of the list in the order presented in the track list. To pause playback in Cover Flow view, tap the Pause symbol in the bottom-left corner of the screen.

To adjust volume in this view, you must move to Play screen view by rotating your iPod to its portrait orientation. When you do, the album cover appears, and you see a volume slider along with play controls (described in the following section).

4. To move to another album, tap the album art icon in the top-right corner of the cover, double-tap an empty spot in the track list, or tap the Information icon in the bottom-right corner of the screen.

Any of these actions flips the track list back to the artwork.

5. To view the contents of a different album from the one you're listening to, flick your finger across the screen to move through your collection.

Go ahead and tap an album or podcast to see its contents. Your selection won't play until you tap a track.

Play screen

Turn your iPod so that it's in portrait orientation, and Cover Flow view disappears (it works only in landscape orientation). What you're left with is the Play screen. This screen is the one you use to perform several tasks, including adjusting volume, navigating through an album, fast-forwarding, switching on shuffle or repeat play, and rating your tracks.

The Play screen has three main views.

Standard Play

The view you see first is straightforward. From the bottom of the screen to the top, you see a volume slider; play controls (including Previous/Rewind, Play/Pause, and Next/Fast Forward); album art; a Back button; Artist, Track Title, and Album title information; and a Track List button (**Figure 2.4**).

Figure 2.4
The music Play screen.

The interface elements function this way:

- The volume slider operates like its real-world equivalent. Just drag the silver ball on the slider to the right to increase volume and to the left to turn the volume down.

- The Previous/Rewind button earns its double name because of its two jobs. Tap it once, and you're taken to the beginning of the currently playing track or chapter of the currently playing podcast or audiobook. Tap twice, and you move to the previous track or chapter. Tap and hold, and the current playing track rewinds.

- The Play/Pause button toggles between these two functions.

- The Next/Fast Forward button works like Previous/Rewind: Tap once to move to the next track in the track list or chapter in an audio-book or podcast; press and hold to fast-forward through the currently playing track.

- Tap the Back button in the top-left corner of the screen, and you move to the currently selected track's view screen. (If you've chosen to view your music by playlist, for example, you see your list of playlists.) When you tap the Back button and are taken to one of these screens, a Now Playing button appears in the top-right corner of the current screen. This button appears whenever you're in the iPod area, making it easy to move to the Play screen.

Track List

In the top-right corner of the Play screen is the Track List button. Tap this button, and you get that album-cover flip effect again and a list of the current album's contents (**Figure 2.5**). (Naturally, if you have only a couple of tracks from that album stored on your iPod, you see just those tracks.) Just as you can in Cover Flow view, you can tap an entry in the track list to listen to that track. Again, tracks play in order from where you tapped.

Figure 2.5
A track list in the music Play screen.

The Track List screen also includes the means for rating tracks. Just above the track list are five gray dots. To assign a star rating from one to five, simply tap one of the dots. (Tap the fourth dot, for example, and the first four dots turn to stars.) You can also wipe your finger across the dots to add or remove stars. These ratings are transferred to iTunes when you next sync your iPod. Tap the artwork image to flip the track list and return to the Play screen.

Additional controls

While you're in the Play screen, tap the artwork in the middle of the screen, and additional controls drop down from above (**FIGURE 2.6**).

Figure 2.6
Additional controls in the music Play screen.

Starting from the left, the first control you'll find is the Repeat button. Tap this button once, and the contents of the currently playing album, audiobook, or podcast repeat from beginning to end. Tap twice, and just the currently playing selection repeats.

A timeline with playhead comes next. To its left is the location of the playhead in minutes and seconds—1:40, for example. To its right is the track's remaining time. Drag the playhead with your finger to move to a different position in the currently playing track.

To the far right is the Shuffle button. When you tap this button once, it turns blue, and the contents of the current album are shuffled. Tap the button again to turn shuffle off.

iPod content views

The iPod's Music area provides several ways to organize your tunes. Look across the bottom of the screen when you're in the iPod area (anywhere but in the Play screen), and you see five buttons for doing just that: Playlists; Artists; Songs; Albums; and More, which leads you to even more options (**Figure 2.7**).

Figure 2.7
Category icons at the bottom of the iPod touch's Music screen.

These buttons are largely self-explanatory. When you tap Playlists, you see a list of all the playlists you've synced to your iPod. Tap a playlist to move to a screen where all the tracks in the playlist appear in the order in which they were arranged in iTunes. If you clicked the Album heading when the playlist was displayed in iTunes, for example, the tracks appear in album order. Tap a track, and you're taken to the Play screen, where the track begins playing.

Whenever you choose a list of tracks in one of these views, Shuffle is the entry at the top of the list. Tap Shuffle, and the contents of that collection of tracks play in random order.

On-The-Go Playlist

The iPod has an On-The-Go playlist—a playlist that you can create directly on the iPod rather than syncing it from iTunes. You can add individual songs or clumps of songs to this special playlist. It works this way:

Tap On-The-Go, and a screen rises up from the bottom of the display, hinting that you've entered a special area of the iPod (**FIGURE 2.8**). Tap one of the entries at the bottom of the screen—Playlists, Artists, Songs, Albums, or More (and then one of the selections available in the More screen). When you do, you see a screen that features the words *Add All Songs* followed by a list of all the songs that belong to that entry (all the songs on an album or by a particular artist, for example). If you tap Add All Songs, you do just that. To add individual songs, tap them. Continue tapping buttons at the bottom of the screen or in the More screen until you've added all the tracks you care to; then tap Done at the top of the screen.

Figure 2.8
Editing the On-The-Go playlist.

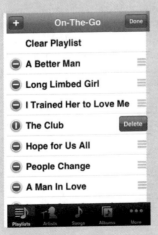

continues on next page

On-The-Go Playlist *continued*

When you return to the Playlists screen and tap On-The-Go, you see a list of all the tracks you've added through your previous endeavors. To edit the contents of this playlist, tap the Edit button in the top-right corner of the screen. In this Edit screen, you can tap the Clear Playlist entry to do just that; tap the minus (–) button next to a track to produce the Delete button, which allows you to remove that track from the playlist (but not from your iPod); or drag the List button to change the position of the selected track in the playlist. While you're in the Edit screen, you can also tap the plus (+) button to add more tracks to your On-The-Go playlist. Tap the plus button and you're back to the view where you can add playlists, artists, songs, and so on.

Tap Artists to see an alphabetical list of the artists represented on your iPod. If your iPod has tracks from more than one album by the selected artist, when you tap the artist's name, you go to an Albums screen that displays the titles of the artist's represented albums (along with thumbnails of the cover art). To view tracks from a particular album, tap its name. To view all songs by the artist, tap All Songs in this screen.

The Songs screen lists all the songs on your iPod. If any list is long (this one included), you see a tiny representation of the alphabet along the right side of the screen. To navigate to a letter quickly, tap it (as best you can, as the letters are really small) or slide your finger along the alphabet listing to dash through the list.

tip If the name of an item in one of these lists begins with *A* or *The*, the item's not filed under *A* or *T*; the following word designates where it's filed. The Beatles are filed under *B*, for example, and "A Case of You" appears under *C*.

When a Video Is Not a Video

In iTunes, you can create a playlist that contains both audio and video. iTunes will warn you that it's not a good idea, but you can still do it. When you sync one of these playlists to your iPod, one of a couple of things happens:

- If the video you added to the playlist is anything but a music video or a video podcast, it won't be synced to the iPod. To sync TV shows and movies, you must choose them in the iPod Preferences Video pane.

- If you've included a music video or a video podcast, it will be synced to your iPod, but it will appear twice. One version appears in the audio playlists. You'll find it in the playlist you created (which appears in the iPod's Playlists screen). When you tap the Artists icon, you'll also see it listed under the artist's name (*Kate Bush*, for example, if it's one of Kate's music videos). It also appears in the Songs screen, listed alphabetically. In the case of a video podcast, it *also* appears in the Podcasts screen. This version will play the video's audio track only, and a frame from the video will be used for the artwork in the Play screen. The version that has actual moving video will appear in the iPod's Video screen, filed under its type: Music Videos or Podcasts.

I know it sounds goofy, but there's a method to this apparent madness. This scheme allows you to enjoy the music in a music video (which presumably is at least part of the reason you have it) when you can't be bothered with video—when you're driving, for example. Same goes with a video podcast. You can listen to the content without having to gaze on a face that's best enjoyed on radio.

The iPod has limited space, yet it gives you many more ways to organize your music—by audiobooks, compilations, composers, and genres, for example. That's exactly what the More button is for. Tap it, and you see just those items, as well as a Podcasts entry. Tap these entries, and most behave pretty much as you'd expect, except for a couple of variations:

- The Compilations entry lists only those albums that have been deemed compilations by iTunes. These items usually are greatest-hits collections, soundtracks, or albums on which lots of artists appear (tribute albums or concert recordings, for example).

- The Podcasts screen displays all the podcasts on your iPod, along with their cover art. If you see a blue dot next to the podcast's name, it means that you have episodes you haven't

More Mucking

Unhappy that Apple chose to tuck the Genres entry in the More screen, yet left Artists easily accessible at all times? No worries. You can change what appears at the bottom of the iPod area. Simply tap More and then tap the Edit button in the top-left corner of the screen. Doing so produces a Configure screen that swipes up from the bottom of the display. Here, you see all the iPod category entries. Find one you like, and drag it over a button at the bottom of the screen that you want to replace. The new entry takes the place of the old one, and the old entry is listed in the More screen. When you're done, tap Done.

listened to yet. Tap a podcast title, and you're taken to a screen that lists all that podcast's episodes. A blue dot next to a podcast episode indicates an unlistened-to episode.

Videos

Like today's display-bearing iPods and the iPhone, the iPod touch plays videos. Some people would say that *unlike* smaller iPods, the iPod touch plays videos that are actually watchable—bright and plenty big enough for personal viewing. Here are the ins and outs of iPod touch video.

Supported video formats

Regrettably, you can't take just any video you pull from the Web or rip from a DVD and plunk it onto your iPod. The iPod has standards that the video must meet before it's allowed to touch your iPod. Specifically, the video must be in either MPEG-4 or H.264 format and must fit within these limits:

MPEG-4
Resolution: 640 by 480
Data rate: up to 2.5 Mbps
Frame rate: 30 fps
Audio: up to 48 kHz

H.264
Resolution: 640 by 480
Data rate: up to 1.5 Mbps
Frame rate: 30 fps
Audio: up to 48 kHz

You can also encode H.264 movies at a resolution of 320 by 240 at 30 fps. When you do so, the data rate is limited to 768 Kbps. *Wha!?*

Don't fret about it. If you spend much time encoding video files, these numbers make sense to you. If not, you needn't bone up on this technology, because iTunes provides a way to make your videos compatible with the iPod. Here's how:

1. Drag an unprotected video onto the Library entry in iTunes' Source list.

   If the video is compatible with iTunes, it's added. If it's not compatible, the icon zips back to its original location.

   Although the video may play in iTunes, if its resolution or data rate is too high, iTunes won't sync it to the iPod.

2. To make a high-resolution or high-data-rate video compatible with the iPod, select it in the Movies or TV Shows category in iTunes' Source list; then choose Advanced > Convert Selection for iPod (**Figure 2.9**).

   This command creates an iPod-compatible version of the video, which you can then sync to your iPod.

Figure 2.9
Convert a
video for iPod
compatibility.

note

This version won't replace the original, so it's not a bad idea to rename the converted version—*Rocky and Bullwinkle (iPod)*, for example—so that you can identify and sync the right one.

Choosing and playing videos

Playing videos on your iPod touch is straightforward. Tap the Videos button at the bottom of the Home screen, and you see your videos listed by categories: Movies, TV Shows, Music Videos, and Podcasts (**Figure 2.10**). Each video has a thumbnail image of its artwork next to it. Depending on the original source of the video, the screen may list Title, Artist, Season, and Episode information. It definitely lists the length of the video—1:56:26, for example.

Figure 2.10
The Videos screen.

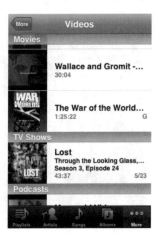

To play a video, tap it. Videos play only in landscape orientation, regardless of which way you have the iPod turned. And unlike in Cover Flow view, videos are always oriented so that they're right-side up, so your iPod is oriented with the Home button on the right.

The video Play screen is similar to the music Play screen except that the play controls and timeline are not visible unless you make them so. To do so, tap the video once (**Figure 2.11**). Play controls (the usual Previous/Rewind, Play/Pause, Next/Fast Forward, and volume-slider controls) appear, as does a time-line near the top of the screen. The volume slider and timeline work just like they do in the audio Play screen. Drag the playhead (represented by the silver dot) to increase or decrease volume or, in the case of the timeline, to move to a new location in the video.

Figure 2.11
The video Play screen.

As I mention earlier, you can advance to the next chapter by tapping the Next/Fast Forward button once. (If the video has no chapters, nothing happens when you tap this button.) If you tap and hold, the video speeds up. To retreat a chapter, tap Previous/Rewind twice (tap once to return to the beginning of the currently playing chapter). The play controls list the chapter you're currently watching—Chapter 13 of 32, for example.

The video Play screen has a control you haven't seen before: the Scale button, in the top-right corner. Tapping this button toggles the display between Fill Screen and Fit to Screen. (You also can toggle these views by double-tapping the display.)

Fill Screen is similar to DVDs you've seen that say the movie was altered to fit your TV. The iPod's entire screen is taken up by video, but some of the content may be chopped off in the process.

Fit to Screen displays the entire video, similar to letterbox-format movies you may have seen. In this view, you may see black bars at the top and bottom or at the sides.

When you finish watching a video, tap the screen; then tap the Done button in the top-left corner. You return to the Videos screen.

tip

The iPod can remember where you last left off. The option for that is in the Video area of the Settings screen. Tap Settings in the Home screen; then tap Videos. In the resulting screen, you see the Start Playing option. Tap it, and you have two choices: Where Left Off and From Beginning. When you next play this video, it will respond accordingly.

Photos

Tapping the third icon at the bottom of the iPod touch's Home screen—the one marked *Photos*—is the digital equivalent of flipping open your wallet to reveal a seemingly endless stream of pictures of the kids, dog, and that recent trip to Pago Pago. For here, you find the pictures you've chosen to sync from your computer.

But this iPod's photo feature is no mere repository for pictures. Flick a finger, and you're flying from photo to photo. If you have a more formal presentation in mind—a viewing of your child's first birthday party for Grandma and Grandpa, for example—you can create something far grander in the form of a slide-show. To learn about these and other photographic wonders, just follow along.

The face of Photos

When you tap Photos, the Photo Albums screen appears. In this screen, you find a couple of entries (and, I hope, eventually more than just a couple).

The first entry is Photo Library, which contains all the photos on your iPod. It bears a thumbnail (not one of your images, but a sunflower), and it displays the total number of images in the library—Photo Library (162), for example. Tap this entry, and in the resulting Photo Library screen, you see thumbnail images of all the photos on your iPod.

As I explain in the iTunes chapter, you can sync photo albums created by such programs as iPhoto, Aperture, Photoshop Elements, and Photoshop Albums. When you do, these albums appear as separate entries in the Photo Albums screen, each featuring a thumbnail from the first image in the album as well as the number of images in the album—Father's Day (48) and Family Holiday (92), for example. When you choose your Pictures folder (Mac), My Pictures (PC), or a folder of your choosing within iTunes' Photos tab, any folders contained within those folders are presented as separate albums. So if in your My Pictures folder, you have three folders that contain pictures—Betty's Birthday, Dog Polisher, and Cheeses Loved and Lost—each of those items will appear as a separate album in the Photo Albums screen. Again, each album title lists, in parentheses, the number of images the album contains.

Picture viewing

Think videos look good on your iPod? Wait until you see photos. The iPod's display is the perfect portable platform for showing off your favorite photos.

As I mention earlier in this chapter, when you're in an album's screen, you see all the pictures in that album arrayed as four-across thumbnail images (**Figure 2.12**). You can see 20 complete thumbnails on the screen. If your album contains more than 20 images, just flick your finger up across the display to scroll more images into view. To see a picture full-screen, just tap it.

Figure 2.12
A photo album's thumbnail images.

Orienteering

For those of you keeping score at home, Photos is one of those areas of the iPod that work in both portrait and landscape orientation. If you have a picture you've taken in a camera's "normal" orientation, your best bet is to flip the iPod to landscape view (**Figure 2.13**).

Figure 2.13
Widescreen
picture view.

All the glorious wide-screen goodness of your picture will be revealed without a large black bar being slapped on either side of your photo. Fond of doing as the pros do and flipping your camera on its side for portraits? Your iPod can accommodate these photos best when you hold the phone in its normal up-and-down orientation.

The iPod automatically rotates and resizes your images to accommodate the phone's orientation. And unlike videos, which display horizontally only when the Home button is on the right side of the screen, photos display in their correct orientation regardless of which way you've turned the iPod: up, down, left, or right.

tip   If you always want to view your photos at their best advantage—horizontal shots viewed in landscape orientation and vertical pictures in portrait orientation—yet you tire of flipping the iPod constantly, try creating photo albums based on picture orientation. Put all your portrait-oriented photos in one album and your favorite landscape shots in another. When the time comes to view them, they'll always look their best without your having to reorient the iPod.

The picture screen

In addition to letting you rotate your pictures by flip-ping your iPod around, the screen in which you view individual images offers some other cool features. When viewing a picture in an album, you briefly see a transparent gray control bar at the bottom of the screen, displaying four symbols: Options, Previous, Play, and Next (**Figure 2.14**). This control bar conveniently disappears after a couple of seconds so that you can see the complete picture without obstruction. To bring it back, just tap the display.

Figure 2.14
The picture screen.

The left- and right-arrow buttons that represent the Previous and Next commands do just what they suggest. Tap the left-arrow button, and you move to the previous image in the album. Tap the right-arrow button, and you're on to the next image. If you tap and hold these buttons, you zip through your pictures at increasing speed. When you tap the Play button, a slideshow begins, starting with the current image and playing to the end.

The timing and transitions of your slideshow are determined by options in the Photos entry in the iPod's Settings screen. You have the option to play each slide for 2, 3, 5, 10, or 20 seconds. Also, you can choose among Cube, Dissolve, Ripple, Wipe Across, and Wipe Down transitions.

At the top of the screen, you briefly see another transparent gray bar. This one has a left-pointing arrow bearing the name of the currently selected photo album. As in most iPod touch screens, you tap this arrow to move up one screen in the iPod's hierarchy. You'll also see an entry such as 8 of 48, which tells you which picture of the total number of pictures you're looking at.

Moving pictures

Tapping those Previous and Next buttons is the less impressive way to move from picture to picture. For a far more stirring demonstration of the iPod's slickness, swipe your finger to the right to advance to the next picture or to the left to retreat one picture. You're guaranteed an "ooh!" from the audience on this one.

While you've got your audience in an "ooh!"ing mood, try this: Double-tap a picture. Like magic, the iPod zooms in on the center of the picture.

Drag your finger on the picture to reposition it. If you'd like greater control of how large the image is, use the stretch gesture to make it grow incrementally. Regrettably, the iPod won't remember how you've repositioned and resized the picture. You also can't swipe to the next picture until you've restored the picture to its original size. You can do this by double-tapping the display again or by pinching the image down to its native size.

Swiping is good any time, even during a slideshow. If, while viewing a slideshow, you'd like to take control, just tap the display to stop the slideshow, or swipe your finger to the left or right to go forward or back, respectively. When you do this, the slideshow moves to that picture, and the slideshow is canceled. To restart it, you must tap the display to produce the play controls and then tap the Play button.

These settings are the defaults. If you've configured the Photo Settings so that the Repeat and Shuffle options are on, the slideshow will behave a bit differently. To begin with, the show will reach the end and then start over, continuing to play until you tell it to stop by tapping the display. And if Shuffle is on, the photos in the selected album will play in random order.

iTunes

The last icon at the bottom of the iPod touch's Home screen is iTunes. When you tap this icon while your iPod is connected to a Wi-Fi network, you're whisked to the iTunes Wi-Fi Music Store—the portable form of Apple's online media emporium. To learn more about the iTunes Wi-Fi Music Store (and its parent, the iTunes Store), please drop by Chapter 5.

Additional applications

As I say early in the chapter, the iPod touch includes applications that handle duties unrelated to media: Safari, YouTube, Calendar, Contacts, Clock, and Calculator. The first four of these applications are covered in more detail elsewhere in the book. Given their mostly limited functionality, I can squeeze Clock and Calculator into an increasingly long chapter in what is supposed to be a smallish book.

Clock

More than just a simple timepiece, the iPod's Clock application includes four components—World Clock, Alarm, Stopwatch, and Timer—that are available as buttons arrayed across the bottom of the application's screen. Here's what they do:

World Clock. Just as its name implies, World Clock allows you to track time in multiple locations. Clocks are presented in both analog and digital form. On analog clocks, day is indicated by a white clock and night by a black one. To add a new clock to the list, just tap the plus button in the top-right corner of the screen; in the resulting keyboard screen, enter the name of a reasonably significant city or a country in the Search field. The iPod includes a database of such cities and offers suggestions as you type.

You can remove or reorder these clocks. Tap Edit, and use the red minus (–) button to delete a clock. Drag clocks up or down the list by the Order icon on the right side of the clock to reposition them.

Alarm. Your iPod can get you out of bed in the morning or remind you of important events. Just tap Alarm at the bottom of the screen and then tap the plus button to add an alarm (**Figure 2.15**).

Figure 2.15
Get up with the iPod touch's alarm clock.

In the Add Alarm screen, you find a Repeat entry, which allows you to order an alarm to repeat each week on a particular day; a Sound entry, which lets you assign one of five sounds to your alarm (Checkmate, Jump, Time Passing, Time's Up, or Up Down); an On/Off Snooze entry, which, when on, tells the iPod to give you 10 more minutes of shuteye when you press the Home button; and a Label entry that allows you to assign a message to an alarm (Get Up, Meeting This Morning, or Drink Your Milk, for example).

To create a new alarm, just flick the hour, minutes, and AM/PM wheels to set a time for the alarm. Tap Save to save the alarm. When you save at least one alarm, a small clock icon appears in the iPod's status bar.

tip

You can create an alarm only for the current 24-hour period. If you'd like an alarm to go off at a time later than that, create an event in your computer's calendar application, attach an alarm to it, and sync the calendar to your iPod. The alarm will transfer with the event.

Stopwatch. The iPod's Stopwatch includes a timer that displays hours, seconds, and tenths of seconds. Tap Start, and the timer begins to run. Tap Stop, and the timer pauses. Tap Start again, and the timer takes up where it left off. Tap Reset, and the timer resets to 00:00.0. While the timer runs, you can tap Lap, and a lap time is recorded in the list below. Subsequent taps of Lap add more lap times to the list. When you tap Lap, the counter resets to 0.

Timer. The iPod's Clock application includes a timer that will tick down from as little as 1 minute to as much as 23 hours and 59 minutes. To work the timer, just use the hour and minute wheels to select the amount of time you'd like the timer to run; then tap Start (**Figure 2.16**). (Alternatively, you can tap a number on the wheel, and it will advance to the "go" position.) The timer displays a countdown in hours, minutes, and seconds. Tap Cancel to stop the countdown.

Figure 2.16
Time keeps on tickin', tickin', tickin' into the future...

The iPod performs one of two actions when the timer ends: Either it plays one of its five built-in sounds through its tiny internal chirping device, or it puts the iPod to sleep. The latter option isn't as odd as it first sounds. Many people like to listen to soothing music or ambient sounds as they drift off to sleep. The Sleep iPod option allows them to do just that without the iPod's playing all night (and, thus, needlessly running down the battery).

Calculator

Unless you've stubbornly clung to your grandfather's abacus, you've used an electronic calculator like this before. Similar to the dime-a-dozen calculators you can find on your computer or at the local Bean Counters-'r'-Us, the iPod's Calculator application performs addition, subtraction, division, and multiplication operations up to nine places. When you choose an operation (addition or subtraction, for example), Calculator highlights that symbol by circling it. In addition to the 0 to 9 digits and the divide, multiply, add, subtract, and equal buttons, you find these buttons:

- **C.** Tap C to clear the total.

- **m+.** Tap m+ to add the displayed number to the number in memory. If no number is in memory, tapping m+ stores the displayed number in memory.

- **m−.** Tap m− to subtract the displayed number from the memorized number.

- **mr/mc.** Tap mr/mc once, and the displayed number replaces the currently memorized number; tap it twice, and memory is cleared. A white ring appears around this button if a number is in memory.

Settings

The iPod touch has a Settings area very much like that of an iPhone. Here, you find preferences that affect the iPod's overall functionality, as well as the performance of specific applications. When you tap the Settings button in the Home screen, this is what you'll find.

Wi-Fi

When you tap the Wi-Fi entry in the Settings screen, you're taken to the Wi-Fi Networks screen (**Figure 2.17**), atop which appears an On/Off switch for enabling or disabling Wi-Fi on your iPod. (Disabling Wi-Fi conserves power.) Below that is the Choose a Network area. Any Wi-Fi networks within range appear in a list below; those that have a lock icon next to them are password protected. To access a password-protected network, simply tap its name, enter the password with the keyboard that appears, and tap Join. To see detailed network information, tap the blue > symbol to the right of the network's name; a new screen appears, listing such information as IP Address, Subnet Mask, Router, DNS, Search Domains, and Client ID.

Tap the Other entry here, and you can enter the name of a hidden network with the iPod keyboard and choose its security protocol: None, WEP, WPA, or WPA2. When you choose a protocol other than None, you also have to enter the network's password.

Figure 2.17
The Wi-Fi
Networks
screen.

 tip   If a network that you never use routinely appears in this list, you can remove it by tapping its name and then tapping Forget This Network in the resulting screen.

Finally, the bottom of the Wi-Fi Networks screen includes the Ask to Join Networks option. Leave the On default setting alone, and your iPod will automatically join known networks and ask to join a network if no known networks are available. If you switch the option off, you'll have to join networks manually without being asked. To do so, tap Other, and enter the name and password (if required) of the network with the keyboard that appears.

Brightness

By default, the iPod's display brightness is adjusted
automatically, based on the light it senses around it.
When you're outdoors on a sunny day, for example,
the screen brightens; when you're in a dark room, the
display dims. If you'd like to override the automatic
brightness settings because the display is too dark
or bright for your taste, you do so in this setting.
Turn autobrightness off, and drag the slider to adjust
brightness up or down.

General

The General settings are...well, pretty general. The
grouping consists of a hodgepodge of controls,
including:

About. This setting provides your iPod's vital statistics: the number of audio tracks, videos, and photos
on the iPod; total capacity; how much storage space
remains; software version; serial and model number;
Wi-Fi address; and a Legal command that, when
tapped, leads to a seemingly endless screen of legal
mumbo-jumbo.

Wallpaper. You see a wallpaper background picture
when you unlock the iPod. To set and adjust your
wallpaper picture, tap the Wallpaper control and
then navigate to an image file in the collection
provided by Apple (listed under the Wallpaper
heading) or among the images you've synced to the
iPod. Just tap the image, and the iPod shows you a
preview of it as wallpaper. You can move the image
by dragging it around or enlarge it by using the

stretch gesture. When you're happy with the picture's orientation, tap Set Wallpaper.

Date & Time. Within the Date & Time screen, you can choose a 24- or 12-hour clock, choose a time zone, and set the date and time manually. (The iPod's date and time are updated automatically whenever you sync the device with your computer.) This screen also has a Calendar area where you can set Time Zone Support to On or Off. As your iPod tells you, "Time Zone Support always shows event dates and time in the time zone selected for calendars. When off, events will display according to the time zone of your current location."

International. The iPod touch is available in a variety of countries, and because it is, it must support languages for those countries. Tap Language in the International screen, and choose among 17 languages. As the iPod touch supports multiple languages, it also must support differing keyboard arrangements for those languages. Tap Keyboards, and choose among the 14 available keyboard layouts. Finally, you can choose the region format—the way dates, time, and phone numbers are displayed. The iPod touch supports 32 region-format schemes.

Auto-Lock. The iPod equivalent of a keypad lock, Auto-Lock tells the touchscreen to ignore taps after a customizable period of inactivity. Use these controls to specify that interval: 1, 2, 3, 4, or 5 minutes, or never. To make the iPod pay attention again, press the Home button.

Passcode Lock. You'd hate to lose your iPod. Worse, you'd hate to lose your iPod and have some ne'er-do-well dig through it for your contacts and schedule. If you fear that your iPod might fall into the wrong hands (and yes, those hands may just belong to your surly teenage daughter), create a passcode. To do so, tap Passcode Lock; then enter and re-enter a four-digit password with the numeric keypad (**FIGURE 2.18**). The next screen offers the option to turn the passcode off (useful if you no longer require a passcode); change the passcode (for...well, you know); and a Require Passcode area, which offers the options Immediately, After 1 Minute, After 5 Minutes, After 15 Minutes, After 1 Hour, and After 4 Hours.

Figure 2.18
The Set
Passcode screen.

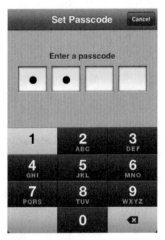

Sound Effects. The iPod can produce sound effects—a tapping sound to accompany keys you type, for example. In this setting, you can turn these effects off or have them emerge from the iPod's tiny speaker, through its headphones, or through both the speaker and headphones.

Keyboard. Care to turn autocapitalization on or off (on means that the iPod automatically capitalizes words after a period, question mark, or exclamation point)? Want to enable or disable Caps Lock (a feature that types in all capitals when you double-tap the keyboard's spacebar)? If so, this setting is for you.

In the Keyboard setting, you also encounter the option to turn the period (.) shortcut on or off. When this option is on, double-tapping the keyboard's spacebar inserts a period and follows it with a space. Finally, this setting includes another instance of the International Keyboards entry that works just as it does in the International setting.

Reset. If you'd like to remove information from your iPod without syncing it to your computer, you use this setting, which provides a variety of options.

The first option, Reset All Settings, resets your iPod's preferences (your Network and Keyboard settings, for example) but doesn't delete media or data (such as your bookmarks or contacts).

If you choose Erase All Content and Settings, the iPod erases your preferences, as well as removes data and media. After you perform this action, you'll need to sync your iPod with iTunes to put this material back on the iPod.

As you type on your iPod's keyboard, word suggestions occasionally crop up. This feature is really handy when the iPod guesses the word you're trying to type. If the word is correct, just tap the spacebar, and the word appears complete onscreen. But if the iPod always guesses particular words incorrectly—your last name, for example—you can correct it by tapping the suggestion and continuing to type. The dictionary will learn that word. When you tap Reset Keyboard Dictionary in the Reset screen, the iPod's dictionary returns to its original state and forgets everything you've taught it.

And to reset the iPod's network settings completely, tap the Reset Network Settings entry.

Fear not that a slip of the finger is going to delete your valuable data. The iPod always pops up a panel that asks you to confirm any Reset choice (FIGURE 2.19).

Figure 2.19
Confirming a reset in the Reset screen.

Music

Like other applications and areas of the iPod, the Music function gets its own little entry in the iPod's Settings screen (**FIGURE 2.20**).

Figure 2.20
The Music Settings screen.

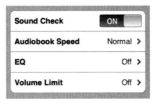

Tap Settings and then iPod, and this is what you see:

Sound Check. iTunes includes a Sound Check feature that you use to make the volumes of all your tracks similar. Without Sound Check, you may be listening to a Chopin prelude at a lovely, lilting volume and be scared out of your socks when the next track, AC/DC's "Highway to Hell," blasts through your brain. When Sound Check is on, each track should be closer to the same relative volume.

The iPod includes an On/Off Sound Check option, but it works only if you've first switched Sound Check on in iTunes; iTunes must evaluate your tracks and set an instruction in each one so that all the tracks work with Sound Check. To enable Sound Check in iTunes, open iTunes' Preferences, click the Playback icon, and enable the Sound Check option. Now when you sync your tracks with the iPod and switch Sound Check on in the iPod's Music Settings screen, you'll experience all that is Sound Check.

Audiobook Speed. The iPod allows you to play tracks designated as Audiobooks at Slower, Normal, or Faster speed. If you have a hard time understanding what the narrator is saying, try Slower. If you're in a hurry, give Faster a shot.

EQ. *EQ* (or *equalization*) is the process of boosting or cutting certain frequencies in the audio spectrum—making the low frequencies louder and the high frequencies quieter, for example. If you've ever adjusted the bass and treble controls on your home or car stereo, you get the idea.

The iPod comes with the same EQ settings as iTunes. Those settings include:

- Off
- Bass Booster
- Classical
- Deep
- Flat
- Jazz
- Loudness
- Piano
- R & B
- Small Speakers
- Treble Booster
- Vocal Booster

- Acoustic
- Bass Reducer
- Dance
- Electronic
- Hip Hop
- Latin
- Lounge
- Pop
- Rock
- Spoken Word
- Treble Reducer

EQ and the iPod

Having EQ built into iTunes and the iPod is great, but the interaction between iTunes and the iPod in regard to EQ is a little confusing. Allow me to end that confusion.

In iTunes, you can assign an EQ setting to songs individually by clicking the song, pressing Command-I (Mac) or Ctrl-I (Windows), clicking the Options tab, and then choosing an EQ setting from the Equalizer Preset menu. When you move songs to your iPod, these EQ settings move right along with them, but you won't be able to use them unless you configure the iPod correctly.

If, for example, you have EQ switched off on the iPod, songs that have assigned EQ presets won't play with those settings. Instead, your songs will play without the benefit of EQ. If you set the iPod's EQ to Flat, the EQ setting that you preset in iTunes will play on the iPod. If you select one of the other EQ settings on the iPod (Latin or Electronic, for example), songs without EQ presets assigned in iTunes will use the iPod EQ setting. Songs with EQ settings assigned in iTunes will use the iTunes setting.

If you'd like to hear how a particular song sounds on your iPod with a different EQ setting, start playing the song on the iPod, press the Home button, tap Settings, tap Music, tap EQ, and then select one of the EQ settings. The song will immediately take on the EQ setting you've chosen, but this setting won't stick on subsequent playback. If you want to change the song's EQ more permanently, you must do so in iTunes.

Although you can listen to each EQ setting to get an idea of what it does, you may find it easier to open iTunes; choose View > Show Equalizer; and, in the resulting Equalizer window, choose the various EQ settings from the window's pop-up menu. The equalizer's ten-band sliders will show you which frequencies have been boosted and which have been cut. Any slider that appears above the o dB line indicates a frequency that has been boosted. Conversely, sliders that appear below o dB have been cut.

Volume Limit. Though Apple takes pains to warn you in the iPod's documentation that blasting music at full volume into your ears can lead to hearing loss, some people just can't get enough volume. If your child is one of those people, consider setting a volume limit on the iPod. To do so, tap Volume Limit in the Music settings screen, and in the resulting Volume Limit screen, use the volume slider to set an acceptable volume. (Having a track playing when you do this is helpful so that you can listen to the effect.) To keep your kid from changing your settings, tap Lock Volume Limit. A Set Code screen will appear, where you'll enter and confirm a four-digit security code. When this code is set, the Lock Volume Limit button changes to Unlock Volume Limit. Tap this button, and you'll be prompted for the security code.

Video

The Video settings screen includes four entries. The first, Start Playing, lets you choose whether videos start where they last left off (in the middle of a video you started watching in iTunes, for example) or always at the beginning.

The second option, Closed Captioning, is an on/off option that, when on, displays closed captioning on programs that support this video feature. (As this book goes to press, no such programs are available, though this option hints that they may become available from the iTunes Store.)

Below these two entries is the TV Out area. The iPod touch can play video on a connected TV with a compatible cable. Older iPod accessories that support video out don't work with the current iPods (the touch, 3G nano, and iPod classic). Instead, you have to purchase a compatible Apple Composite Video Cable or Component Video Cable (each costs $49) or a modern Made for iPod–branded accessory that hosts Apple's proprietary iPod authorization chip.

The TV Out options allow you to choose Widescreen on/off (on is widescreen, and off is standard TV view, in which the picture fills the screen but the left and right edges are cut off) and to specify whether the TV signal is NTSC (the video standard in the United States) or PAL (the standard for Europe and Australia).

Photos

The Photos setting is where you configure the Photos application's slideshows. Options include how long each slide appears onscreen (2, 3, 5, 10, or 20 seconds), the transition between slides (Cube, Dissolve, Ripple, Wipe Across, or Wipe Down), Repeat (on/off), and Shuffle (an on/off setting for playing slides in random order).

Safari

In the Safari setting's General area, you can choose which search engine the Web browser uses: Google or Yahoo. In the Security screen, you can choose to run JavaScript (bits of code that enhance Web pages by allowing you to use interactive elements such as buttons and embedded menus) and plug-ins (add-on doodads that let you do things like view QuickTime movies in a Web page). You can also choose to block pop-up windows.

Additionally, you can determine how cookies (bits of code planted by a Web site on your computer or an Internet device such as the iPhone or iPod touch) are treated. You can choose to never accept cookies, accept them from just the site you're visiting, or always accept them.

Near the bottom of the Safari settings screen, you find Clear History, Clear Cookies, and Clear Cache buttons. Tap each button to perform the task it suggests. (I talk more about the benefits of tapping these buttons in Chapter 6.)

Finally, you find a Developer button at the very bottom of the screen. Tap this button to go to the Developer screen, where you can choose to turn a debug console on or off. When it's switched on, this console provides details on any Web-page errors it encounters. (Unless you're a geek, leave this option off, as the console takes up a significant amount of space onscreen when you use Safari.)

Contacts

This final setting lets you choose the sort order and display order of your contacts: First, Last or Last, First.

3

The "Traditional" iPods

As I try to make clear in Chapter 2, the iPod touch and the "traditional" iPods—today's iPod nano, iPod classic, and iPod shuffle—are completely different animals. The iPod touch lacks physical controls; the nano and classic sport the click wheel we've grown to know and love; and the shuffle's wheel doesn't click. The touch invites tapping and flicking; the traditional iPods, wheeling and pressing. In this chapter, I direct your attention to these wheel-bearing iPods.

On the Face of It

On the front of your iPod classic and iPod nano, you'll find a display and set of navigation controls. The shuffle dispenses with the display and provides a simplified set of controls. On the first two generations (1G and 2G) of the iPod, these controls were arrayed around a central scroll wheel and were mechanical—meaning that they moved and activated switches underneath the buttons. On the third-generation (3G) iPods, these controls were placed above the scroll wheel and were touch sensitive; they activated when they came into contact with your flesh but, allegedly, not when a nonfleshy object (such as the walls of your backpack, pocket, or purse) touched them.

The iPod mini, fourth-generation (4G) and later full-size iPods, and the iPod nano bear a click wheel that incorporates the navigation buttons. Unlike the first two generations of the iPod, on which the buttons are arrayed around the outside of the wheel, these buttons are part of the wheel itself (**Figure 3.1**). Their sensors sit beneath the wheel at the four compass points, and the scroll wheel sits on a short spindle that allows it to rock in all directions. To activate one of the buttons, just press the wheel in the direction of that button.

Figure 3.1
iPod's click wheel.

The iPod shuffle's navigation controls are based on this wheel idea but don't duplicate it exactly. The ring around the center button is far narrower than you'll find on the mama and papa iPods, and it functions somewhat differently. Because of the shuffle's lack of a display and different controls, I discuss it separately.

The iPod display

Near the top of the iPod classic sits a 2.5-inch-diagonal, color liquid crystal display that can show up to 65,536 colors at a resolution of 320 by 240 pixels. Like the nano, the standard iPod display features backlighting (illumination that makes the display easier to read in dim light), which you can switch on simply by touching the click wheel (with older iPods you switch on backlighting by pressing the Menu button). By default, the backlight is configured to shine for 10 seconds.

Measured diagonally, the color display of the 3G nano is half an inch smaller than that of the iPod classic, yet it projects as much text and video as its larger sibling. It does this by using a different font from the one used on the iPod classic, as well as greater pixel density (meaning that it packs more pixels per inch on the screen).

iPod and iPod nano controls

The controls of the iPod classic and 3G iPod nano are identical, so it makes sense to discuss them together.

Play/Pause button

If you scan the surface of your iPod classic or 3G iPod nano, you'll notice that it bears no recognizable On/Off switch. To switch on current iPod classics and iPod nanos, press the Center button. (This same technique works with the fifth-generation, or 5G, iPod and the 1G and 2G iPod nanos.) On models earlier than the 5G iPod, start up by using the Play/Pause button. To switch off any display-bearing iPod, press and hold its Play/Pause button for about 3 seconds. This button is located at the bottom of the iPod control wheel on older iPods, in the third position in the row of buttons on 3G iPods, and at the bottom of the click wheel on today's iPod classic and iPod nano. As you'd expect, pressing this button also starts and pauses music, video playback, and photo slideshows.

Previous button

This button is located on the far-left side of the wheel on 1G, 2G, and click-wheel iPods; it's the far-left button on 3G iPods. In most cases, pressing this button once takes you to the beginning of the currently playing song or video.

Movies purchased from the iTunes Store are the exception. If these movies have chapter marks (and all do, as far as I know), pressing Previous moves the movie to the previous chapter. Press Previous multiple times to move back multiple chapters. If you've pressed Previous more times than the movie has chapters, you're taken back to the Movies screen. Pressing Previous twice in succession in a music play-list moves you to the previous song in the playlist. Do this with a video track, and you're taken back to the Video screen or that video's playlist screen. Hold down Previous to rewind through a song, video, or movie. When you rewind or fast-forward through a song, video, or movie, you move in small increments at first. As you continue to hold the button down, you move in larger increments.

On iPods with a color display, the Previous button also moves you back through a slideshow.

Next button

Look to the far right on 1G, 2G, and click-wheel iPods; look to the rightmost button on 3G iPods. This button behaves similarly to the Previous button. Press it when viewing a movie to move forward through chapters. Press this button once to go to the next song in a music playlist. Press it once while viewing a nonmovie video, and you're returned to the Video screen or that video's playlist screen. Hold Next down to fast-forward through a song, video, or movie. As is true of rewinding, fast-forwarding moves you through small increments of a song or video at first. As you continue to hold the button down, the increments get larger.

On iPods with a color display, the Next button advances you through a slideshow.

Menu button

Pressing the well-marked Menu button takes you back through the interface the way you came. If you've moved from the main iPod screen to the Browse screen, for example, and you press the Menu button, you'll move back to the main iPod screen. If you've moved from the main iPod screen through the Playlist screen to a particular song within a particular playlist, each time you press the Menu button, you'll move back one screen.

On iPods earlier than the iPod classic and 3G iPod nano, holding the Menu button down for about 2 seconds turns backlighting on or off.

Scroll wheel

Inside the ring of buttons on 1G and 2G iPods, below the bevy of buttons on 3G iPods, and marked with the navigation controls on click-wheel iPods is the scroll wheel. Moving your thumb clockwise highlights items below the selected item; moving the wheel counterclockwise highlights items above the selected item. If a window is larger than the display, moving the scroll wheel causes the window to scroll up or down when the first or last item in the list is highlighted.

You also use the scroll wheel to adjust volume and to move to a particular location in a song, video, or movie.

Center button

The bull's-eye of all iPods—the Center button—
selects a menu item. If the Settings menu item is
selected, for example, pushing the Center button
moves you to the Settings screen, where you can
select additional settings.

When you press the Center button while a song is
playing and the Play screen is visible, you move to
another Play screen, where you can *scrub* (quickly
navigate forward and back with the scroll wheel)
your song or video. On the iPod classic and 3G nano,
press this button again to move to the Ratings
screen, where you can assign a rating of one to five
stars to the song by using the scroll wheel. Press
Center yet again, and the Shuffle screen appears,
where you can tell the iPod to shuffle playback by
Songs or Albums (or not at all, if another shuffle
setting has been selected). If you've added lyrics to
the song in iTunes (more on this in Chapter 4), one
more press of the Center button displays those lyrics
in the next screen.

While you're watching a movie with chapter marks,
pressing the Center button once displays a progress
bar that includes the movie's chapter marks. Press
the button again, and the scrub control appears.
Press one more time, and a brightness bar appears.
Just thumb the click wheel up or down to adjust
brightness.

iPod shuffle status light and controls

There's no need to mention the shuffle's display, because it has none. It does have a status light that tells you what it's doing, however, as well as navigation controls on the front. The 2G and 3G models also have power and play-order switches on the bottom, and the 1G shuffle has a single power/play-order switch on the back. Here's how they work.

Status light

The top and bottom of the 2G and 3G iPod shuffles include small LEDs. When you first turn on a charged shuffle, a light glows green on these LEDs for about 3 seconds. When you press Play or any part of the outer ring, the green light briefly appears again. If you pause playback, the green light blinks for just under a minute. When you lock the shuffle, an amber status light blinks three times rapidly. Press any of the controls while the shuffle is locked, and you'll see this same amber glow.

When you plug the shuffle into a power source, its amber light will glow continuously and then switch to the green LED when the shuffle is fully charged.

Outer ring

The ring that surrounds the inner Play/Pause button handles track "navigation" (such as it is) and volume control (**Figure 3.2**). Press the top part of the ring (marked with a +) to increase volume. Press the bottom of the ring (marked with a –) to turn the volume down. The right side of the ring controls the iPod's Next function; press once to move to the next track, or press and hold to fast-forward through the currently playing track.

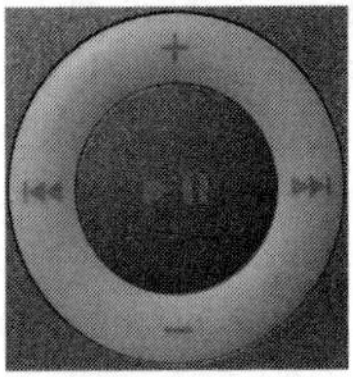

Figure 3.2
iPod shuffle's control wheel.

The Previous button on the left side of the ring works like the Previous buttons on other iPods. Press once, and the currently playing song starts at the beginning. Press twice quickly in succession to move to the previous song in the playlist.

Play/Pause button

Yes, the Play/Pause button does what it says. With the shuffle switched on, press the button once to play; press it again to pause.

Because the shuffle has so few controls, Apple has pressed this button into service to perform other jobs. To go to the beginning of a playlist, for example, press Play/Pause three times quickly (within a second). To lock the iPod (disable its buttons), press and hold the button for about 3 seconds. To unlock it, press and hold the button again.

When you lock the shuffle, its status light blinks three times. When you unlock it, the light briefly glows green.

Power and play-order switches

The top of the shuffle has two switches: one for power and another that toggles between Repeat and Shuffle modes (**FIGURE 3.3**). Push the power switch to the right to turn the shuffle on. Push the play-order switch to the left, and the iPod lives up to its name and shuffles its playlist randomly. Push this switch to the right, and the shuffle plays its playlist, in order, from beginning to end before repeating.

Figure 3.3
iPod shuffle's power and play-order switches.

Battery-status button/light

Unlike the previous iPod shuffle, which carried its own battery status light, the 2G and 3G iPod shuffles indicates their current charge through the LEDs on the top and bottom of the player. To see how much charge you have left, quickly flick the power switch off and then on. The shuffle will continue playing if you do this rapidly enough. A green-glowing LED indicates a full charge (even after the shuffle has played for several hours). If you see an amber light, the shuffle is low on power. A red light indicates that it's *really* low on power, and no light at all tells you that the shuffle is completely drained and should be plugged into a power source to charge.

Ports and connectors: Dock-connector iPods

The iPod doesn't work by osmosis. You need a hole for the sound to get out (and, in some cases, in) and another hole for moving data on and off the device. Here's what you'll find on the Dock-connector iPods.

Headphone jack and Hold switch

The 3G and all click-wheel iPods except the iPod nano, 5G iPod, and iPod classic sport a Headphone jack, a Hold switch, and an iPod Remote Control connector up top (**Figure 3.4** and **Figure 3.5**). You'll find the 3G iPod nano's Hold switch and Headphone port on the bottom (**Figure 3.6**).

Figure 3.4
Top of the
4G iPod.

Figure 3.5
Top of the
iPod mini.

Figure 3.6
Bottom of the
3G iPod nano.

Today's iPods have no Remote Control port. The Headphone jack and Hold switch provide audio output and disable the iPod's controls, respectively, working nearly the same way on today's iPod and iPod nano as they do on older models.

tip I say *nearly* because the Headphone jack, in combination with the Remote Control connector on 3G-and-later standard iPods up to the 5G iPod, supports not only audio output, but also audio input. With a compatible microphone, you can record low-quality audio (8 kHz) on these iPods. Display-bearing iPods—including the 5G iPod, 2G iPod nano, and later iPods—support higher-resolution audio recording via their Dock Connector ports and a compatible microphone.

note The 5G iPod can also transmit composite video via its Headphone jack with a compatible cable. The iPod classic, 3G iPod nano, and iPod touch can transmit composite or component video from their Dock Connector ports with a compatible accessory or cable.

Dock Connector port

On the bottom of a Dock-connector iPod, you'll find a proprietary port that handles both power and data chores for the device. This port, on the bottom of the 3G iPods and all click-wheel iPods save the iPod nano and the 5G iPod, supports data transfer via both FireWire and USB 2.0 (**FIGURE 3.7**). All nanos and the 5G iPod, iPod classic, and iPod touch can be charged via FireWire but sync only over USB.

Figure 3.7
Bottom of the
iPod classic.

Ports and connectors: iPod shuffle

The iPod shuffle has exactly one hole: the Headphone port (**Figure 3.8**). On the original iPod shuffle, this port is exactly what its name implies: a place to plug in your earbuds or other headphones.

Figure 3.8
2G iPod shuffle's Headphone/ Dock port.

Photo courtesy of Apple, Inc.

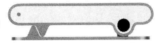

The 2G and 3G iPod shuffles' Headphone port serves two purposes: You not only listen to music through this port, but also sync and charge the iPod through it via the shuffle's Dock. To charge or sync your shuffle, plug the Dock cable into a powered USB 2.0 port on your computer; then slip the shuffle into the Dock so that that its Headphone port slides over the Dock's miniplug.

The original shuffle charges and syncs differently. Flip this shuffle over, pull off its protective cap, and spy the USB connector (**Figure 3.9**). Plug that into your computer's powered USB 2.0 port to charge the iPod and then transfer music and data to it.

Figure 3.9
USB connector at the bottom of the 1G iPod shuffle.

Navigating the Screens

Considering how easy the iPod is to use, it's hard to believe the number of navigation screens that make up its interface. In the following pages, I scrutinize each screen. With the introduction of the iPod classic and 3G iPod nano, both the middle-sized and semi-jumbo iPods have the exact same interface.

Main screen

The main screen (**Figure 3.10**), which displays the word *iPod* at the top, is your gateway to the iPod. In a way, it's akin to the Mac's Finder or Windows' My Computer window—a place to get started.

Figure 3.10
The iPod's main screen.

The main screen on today's traditional iPods contains these commands:

- Music
- Videos
- Photos
- Podcasts
- Extras
- Voice Memos (if you've recorded any with a compatible microphone)
- Settings
- Shuffle Songs
- Now Playing (if a song is playing or paused)

The iPod classic and 3G iPod nano offer a split-screen view (previous iPods list commands only). These commands are arrayed along the left side of the display, and different graphics appear on the right side of the display; the kind of graphic you see depends on which command you've selected. If Music is selected, and you've synced album art to the iPod, album covers swoop across the display. Choose Videos, and similarly swooping still images from the movies, TV shows, music videos, and video podcasts on your iPod appear in this area.

 If, in iTunes, you've chosen to not sync artwork to your iPod, selecting Music or Videos displays a gray screen on the right side of the display that details the number of songs or videos, respectively, on the iPod.

Here's what you'll find within each area.

Music

When you choose the Music command and press the Center button, the resulting Music screen reveals these entries: Cover Flow, Playlists, Artists, Albums, Songs, Genres, Composers, Audiobooks, and Search (**Figure 3.11**). I explain the purposes of all these entries in the following sections.

Figure 3.11
iPod's Music
screen.

Cover Flow

As I mention in Chapter 2, the iPod touch (like iTunes)
includes a Cover Flow view—a way to view your
music collection by album cover. The iPod classic and
3G iPod nano have a similar feature. Select Cover
Flow and press the Center button, and you'll see your
iPod's music collection as a series of album covers,
arranged by the artists' first names (**Figure 3.12**).
Swirl your finger around the click wheel to move
through the album covers. When you find one you
like, press the Center button; the cover flips around
to reveal the tracks it contains.

Figure 3.12
Cover Flow view.

Use the usual scrolling gesture to move down the list
of tracks to select the one you want; then press the
Center button to play it. When you do, the track will
appear in the iPod's Now Playing screen, where you
can adjust its volume and perform the tricks you can
do in any other Now Playing screen. The one difference is that when you press the Menu button, you
return to Cover Flow view rather than go back to an
album screen or menu. To leave Cover Flow view, just
press Menu; you'll return to the Music screen.

Playlists

Regardless of which iPod you're using, when you choose Playlists and press the Center button, you'll see a screen that contains the playlists you have downloaded to your iPod (**Figure 3.13**). Unlike earlier iPods, the iPod classic and 3G iPod nano provide not only the names of the playlists, but also the number of songs each playlist contains.

Figure 3.13
Playlists screen.

Also unlike with earlier iPods, if you've created a folder in iTunes and placed multiple playlists in that folder, that folder hierarchy is present on the iPod as well. If I create a folder called Great 50s Jazz and place my Miles Davis, John Coltrane, and Bill Evans playlists in that folder, when I sync the Great 50s Jazz folder to my iPod, it will appear in the Playlists screen. When I select it and press the Center button, the playlists associated with these jazz greats appear in the resulting screen.

These playlists are created and configured in iTunes. How you configure them is up to you. You may want to gather all your polka favorites in one playlist and put ska in another. Or if you have an iPod shared by

the family, Dad may gather his psychedelic songs of
the '6os in his personal playlist, whereas sister Sue
creates a playlist full of hip-hop and house music.
When I discuss iTunes and other music applications
in later chapters, I'll look at additional approaches for
putting together playlists.

After you select a playlist and press the Center button,
the songs within that playlist appear in a scrollable
screen, and the name of the playlist appears at the
top of the screen. Just select the song you want to
play (new to the latest iPods is the addition of the
artist's name below the song title, as you see in
FIGURE 3.14), and press the Center button. When you
do, you'll move to the Now Playing screen (**FIGURE 3.15**),
which displays the number of songs in the playlist,
the name of the song playing, the artist, and the
name of the album from which the song came.

Figure 3.14
Songs in a
playlist.

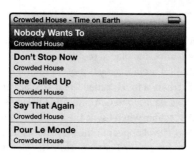

Figure 3.15
Now Playing
screen.

On color iPods and iPod nanos, you'll also see a picture of the album cover if the song has this information embedded in it and iTunes' Display Album Artwork on Your iPod option is enabled. (Monochrome iPods don't display album artwork.) Also appearing in this screen are two timer displays: elapsed time and remaining time. The screen also contains a graphic thermometer display that gives you a visual representation of how far along you are in the song.

note

Text that runs off the screen in the Song, Artist, and Album screens is treated differently on color iPods and the iPod nano than it is on other iPods. Earlier iPods and the iPod mini place an ellipsis (...) at the end of an entry that exceeds the width of the screen. A color-display iPod will scroll selected text from right to left if it's longer than the screen can accommodate.

Additional screens lie beyond the Now Playing screen, one reached by using the scroll wheel and the others by pressing the Center button. If you turn the scroll wheel, you'll move to a screen nearly identical to the Now Playing screen where you can adjust the iPod's volume. Turn clockwise, and you'll raise the volume; turn counterclockwise to lower it.

If you press the Center button while you're in the Now Playing screen, you'll be able to scrub through the song. Like the Now Playing screen, the scrub screen carries a thermometer display that indicates the playing location with a small diamond (**FIGURE 3.16**). Just move your finger across the scroll wheel to start scrubbing. Stop pushing your digit across the scroll wheel in either of these screens, and you'll return to Now Playing after a couple of seconds.

Figure 3.16
Now Playing
screen's scrub
control.

Recent display-bearing iPods include additional screens beyond the scrub screen. On these iPods:

- Press the Center button twice while you're in the Now Playing screen to go the Ratings screen. Use the scroll wheel to assign ratings from one to five stars.

- Press the Center button three times, and you arrive at the Shuffle screen, where you find three options: Off, Songs, and Albums. Use the scroll wheel to move among these options, and press the Center button to select one.

- If you've added lyrics to a track with iTunes 5 or later, pressing the Center button four times in the Now Playing screen takes you to a Lyrics screen.

On-The-Go (Dock-connector iPods)

Scroll to the bottom of the Playlists screen on a Dock-connector iPod, and you'll find an additional playlist that you didn't create: the On-The-Go playlist (**Figure 3.17**).

Figure 3.17
The On-The-Go screen lets you create custom playlists directly on the iPod.

Introduced with iPod Software 2.0 Updater, this playlist is a special one that you create directly on the iPod. It's particularly useful when you need to create a new playlist *right now* and don't have a computer you can plug your iPod into. It works this way:

1. Select a song, artist, playlist, or album.

2. Hold down the Center button until the selected item flashes a few times.

   This flashing indicates that the item has been added to the On-The-Go playlist.

3. Repeat this procedure for any other songs, artists, playlists, and albums you want to add to the list.

4. When you're ready to play your selections, choose On-The-Go from the Playlists screen, and press the Center button.

In the resulting On-The-Go screen, you'll see a list of songs you've added to the list, in the order in which you added them. (The song, artist, playlist, or album you selected first will appear at the top of the list.)

5. Press the Center button to begin playing the playlist.

To save an On-The-Go playlist, just select Save Playlist in the On-The-Go screen and press the Center button. The first playlist will be called New Playlist 1. After you've saved an On-The-Go playlist, you can create another (and likewise save it). To clear the On-The-Go playlist, choose Clear Playlist in this same screen, and press the Center button. A confirmation dialog box appears, letting you choose Clear or Cancel (which you select with the scroll wheel and then confirm by pressing the Center button).

On-The-Go playlists for the previous generation of display-bearing iPods work a little differently. To save an On-The-Go playlist, you scroll down to the bottom of that playlist, choose Save Playlist, and press the Center button. You'll be asked to confirm your choice in a succeeding screen. You use this same method to clear an On-The-Go playlist, as a Clear Playlist command also appears in the On-The-Go screen.

On the click-wheel iPods running the latest iPod Software Updater, Apple expands the On-The-Go playlist's capabilities, allowing you to create multiple On-The-Go playlists on your iPod. To do so, follow these steps:

1. Follow the preceding steps to create an On-The-Go playlist.

2. Scroll to the On-The-Go entry in the Playlists screen, and press the Center button.

   The songs you added to your playlists appear in the On-The-Go screen.

3. Scroll to the bottom of the On-The-Go screen, select Save Playlist, and press the Center button.

4. In the resulting Save screen, scroll to Save Playlist, and press the Center button.

   Your playlist will be saved as New Playlist 1. Each time you save a new On-The-Go playlist, it will be called New Playlist and assigned a number one greater than the last New Playlist created.

When you synchronize your click-wheel iPod with iTunes, your saved On-The-Go playlists will appear successively numbered in iTunes, bearing the name *On-The-Go:* On-The-Go 1, On-The-Go 2, and (you guessed it) On-The-Go 3, for example. During synchronization, these On-The-Go playlists are removed from the iPod. If you'd like them to remain on the iPod, you must direct iTunes to sync them back to the iPod (more on this in Chapter 4).

Artists

The Artists screen displays the names of any artists on your iPod (**FIGURE 3.18**). Choose an artist's name and press the Center button, and you'll be transported to that artist's screen, where you have the opportunity to play every song on your iPod by that artist (by choosing All Songs) or to select a particular album by that artist.

Figure 3.18
Artists screen.

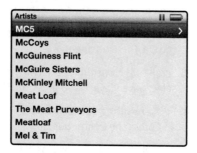

You'll also spy the All Albums entry at the top of the Artists screen. Should you choose this entry, you'll be taken to the All Albums screen, where you can select all albums by all artists. The All Albums screen contains an All Songs command of its own. Select this command, and you'll move to the All Songs screen, which lists all songs by all artists on your iPod. (But if a song doesn't have an Artists entry, the song won't appear in this screen.)

Albums

Choose the Albums entry and press the Center button, and you'll see every album on your iPod (**FIGURE 3.19**). Choose an album and press the Center button to play the album from beginning to end.

The Albums screen also contains an All Songs entry, which, when selected, displays all the songs on all the albums on your iPod. (If the song doesn't have an Albums entry, it won't appear in this screen.)

Figure 3.19
Albums screen.

 An album entry can contain a single song. As long as the album field has been filled in for a particular song within iTunes or another iPod-compatible application (I discuss this topic in Chapter 4), that song will appear in the Albums screen.

Songs

Choose Songs and press the Center button, and you'll see a list of all the songs on your iPod (**FIGURE 3.20**).

Figure 3.20
Songs screen.

Genres

The iPod has the capability to sort songs by genre: Acoustic, Blues, Reggae, and Techno, for example. If a song has been tagged with a genre entry, you can choose it by genre in the Genres screen (**Figure 3.21**). On the 3G nano and iPod classic, below each genre entry, you'll see the number of artists and albums that belong to that genre—*6 Artists, 9 Albums*, for example.

Figure 3.21
Genres screen.

Composers

The iPod can also group songs by composers. This feature, added in iPod Software 1.2 Updater, allows you to sort classical music more easily (**Figure 3.22**). In the Composers screen, you'll see an All Albums screen as well as composers' names. Select All Albums and press the Center button, and all the albums that have been tagged with a composer's name will appear in the resulting All Albums screen.

Figure 3.22
Composers
screen.

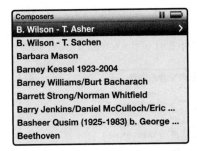

Composers	‖ ▭
B. Wilson - T. Asher	›
B. Wilson - T. Sachen	
Barbara Mason	
Barney Kessel 1923-2004	
Barney Williams/Burt Bacharach	
Barrett Strong/Norman Whitfield	
Barry Jenkins/Daniel McCulloch/Eric ...	
Basheer Qusim (1925-1983) b. George ...	
Beethoven	

Audiobooks

The iPod is capable of playing audiobook files purchased from Audible.com and the iTunes Store. These audiobooks can be identified by their extension: .aa for books bought from Audible.com or .m4b for those bought from the iTunes Store. When an iPod stores one of these specially formatted files, the audiobook's name appears in the iPod's Audiobooks screen (which appears when you choose the Audiobooks command in the Music screen and press the Center button).

Search

When Apple released the updated 5G iPod and 2G iPod nano in late 2006, it gave them a new Search feature. Search is also available on today's 3G iPod nano and iPod classic. On today's iPods, select Search and press the Center button, and you'll see a Search screen. Using the scroll wheel, you scroll through an alphabetical list (the 5G iPod and 2G iPod nano's Search includes both letters and numbers). When you reach the letter you seek, press the Center button to enter that letter in the Search field. When you do this, a list of matching items appears in the top part of the screen (**Figure 3.23**).

Figure 3.23
Searching for items on the iPod.

Continue scrolling and clicking to enter more characters to narrow your search. To remove an unwanted character, press the Previous button to erase the last character you entered. When you've entered as many characters as you care to, select Done on the 5G iPod and 2G iPod nano, and press the Center button. On a 3G nano or iPod classic, just press Menu to exit search. Doing so takes you to the Search Results screen, where you'll see a list of all albums, artists, and songs that contain the character sequence you entered. (Search doesn't work for videos or movies.) Scroll to the item you want, and press the Center button to select it.

If you select a song, it starts playing. If you select an album or artist, you'll see an Albums or Artists screen, and you can continue selecting items and pressing the Center button until you get exactly the track you want.

note **The Search feature is smarter than you may think. Although the list of results generally begins with the first letter you've entered, that list can also contain entries that contain the letters you've entered within the body of the item. Entering *DC*, for example, produces not only AC/DC as an artist entry, but also selections that contain the word *podcast*.**

All 5G iPods (with the latest iPod software), the 2G and 3G iPod nano, and the iPod classic support one other kind of searching. Navigate to the Artists, Albums, Songs, or Composers screen, and start scrolling. In short order, a square gray overlay appears in the middle of the screen, including the letter that reflects where you are in the list. If you're scrolling through the Jack Johnson, Jackie Gleason, Jackie Wilson, James Brown, Janis Joplin, and Jayhawks section of your Artists screen, you'll see the letter *J* overlaid as you scroll.

Videos

Not surprisingly, on traditional iPods, the Videos command is available only on those iPods that are capable of playing video—which, as this book goes to press, are the 5G iPod, the iPod classic, and the 3G iPod nano. Within the Videos screen, you'll find this list of entries.

Movies

Within iTunes, you can tag a video as a Movie, Music Video, or TV Show (I tell you how in Chapter 4). Any video that has the Movie tag assigned to it will show up in the list that appears when you select Movies in the Videos screen and press the Center button.

TV Shows

At the risk of repeating myself, this tag works the same way as the Movie tag. If you have programs tagged as TV Shows, they appear in this list.

Music Videos

This tag works the same way as Movie. Tag a video as a Music Video in iTunes, and it appears in the Music Videos list.

Video Playlists

As I explain in the next chapter, you can create playlists that contain videos and then copy these playlists (and their contents) to a compatible iPod. When you do, those playlists appear when you select Video Playlists in the Videos screen and press the Center button. Select a playlist and press the button again, and you'll see a list of the videos contained in that playlist. Select an item in the playlist and press the Center button or Play, and the selected video will play.

note

It's quite possible to have playlists appear in the Video Playlists screen that contain no video whatsoever. If you have a smart playlist that contains episodes of a particular TV show, but you've told iTunes to sync only unwatched episodes to the iPod and you've watched every episode of the show, the playlist will appear, but it will list no episodes, because iTunes is doing exactly what you told it to: syncing only unwatched episodes. When you add an unwatched episode to iTunes, that episode will sync to the iPod and appear in this playlist.

Settings (Video Settings on 5G iPod, 3G iPod nano, and iPod classic)

Select this command in the Videos screen on a 3G nano or iPod classic and press the Center button, and you'll see four options: TV Out, TV Signal, Fullscreen, and Captions.

You use TV Out to tell the iPod whether to output its video signal via the Headphone jack (the 5G iPod outputs video from the jack with the assistance of Apple's AV cable) or the Dock Connector port on a 3G iPod nano or iPod classic. Off means no signal. Ask means that when you call up a video on the iPod and press Play to begin the show, a screen will appear, asking you whether you'd like the TV signal turned on or left off. On means that the iPod will automatically send the signal out the Dock Connector port on a 3G iPod nano and iPod classic, and out the Headphone jack on a 5G iPod.

The world has two major television standards: NTSC (United States and Japan) and PAL (Europe and Australia). You can choose either for your iPod's video output with the TV Out command.

Fullscreen offers On or Off. Select Off to view wide-screen movies in their native letterbox format. Choose On, and the iPod will scale the picture (and chop off either end) so that it fills the iPod's screen or the screen of the TV it's attached to.

The iPod nano and iPod classic support closed-captioned videos, which I assume will eventually be sold by the iTunes Store (but none are available as this book goes to press). This option turns closed captioning on or off.

The 5G iPod lists just three commands: TV Out, TV Signal, and Widescreen. The only difference is that Widescreen is the default on the 5G iPod. Turning it on displays video in letterbox view; turn it off, and you enter full-screen view.

Photos (color-display iPods only)

The Photos command appears only on iPods with color displays (**Figure 3.24**). This command is your avenue for viewing pictures on your iPod, as well as configuring how slideshows are displayed on it and (if you have a full-size color iPod) on an attached television or projector.

Figure 3.24
The Photos entry.

At the top of the Photos screen, you'll find an All Photos command. Select it and press the Center button to see thumbnail images of every photo stored on the iPod. Use the scroll wheel to select an image. When you select an image, the date when it was taken appears at the top of the display on the 3G nano and iPod classic. To display the image in full-screen view, press the Center button. To move to the next or previous image, press the Next and Previous buttons, respectively. To play a slideshow of your images from the point where you selected an image, press the Play/Pause button. To leave the slideshow, press Menu.

The Photos screen also contains a list of any photo albums you've synced to the iPod via iTunes. (I talk about photo albums and iTunes in Chapter 4.) When you select an album on the 3G iPod nano or iPod classic, images from that album swoop across the right side of the split-screen display.

Additionally, the Photos screen includes a Settings command. Select it and press the Center button, and you'll see these commands:

Time Per Slide. You can configure the iPod so that slideshows are under manual command and you need to press the Next or Previous button to navigate the slideshow. You can also have the iPod change slides automatically every 2, 3, 5, 10, or 20 seconds.

Music. Your slideshow can be accompanied by music. In the Slideshow Music screen, choose Now Playing, Off, one of the playlists on the iPod, or the On-The-Go playlist.

Repeat. If you like, you can have your slideshow repeat forever (or at least until the iPod runs out of power). This command is a simple On/Off command.

Shuffle Photos. This command is another On/Off command. Off means that your slides play in order; choose On, and they're displayed randomly.

Transitions. The color iPods offer built-in *transitions* (effects that occur when you move from one slide to another). The included effects on the 3G iPod nano and iPod classic are Random (a random mix of effects), Cross Fade, Fade to Black, Zoom Out, Wipe Across, and Wipe Center. The 5G iPod offers a broader set of transitions, including Random, Cube Across, Cube Down, Dissolve, Page Flip, Push Across, Push Down, Radial, Swirl, Wipe Across, Wipe Down, and Wipe from Center.

TV Out (including 5G iPod, 3G iPod nano, and iPod classic). This command works just as it does for video settings.

tip

Turning on TV output depletes the battery charge in a big way. Switch this option on only if you really need it.

TV Signal (including 5G iPod, 3G iPod nano, and iPod classic). Same here. Your options are NTSC and PAL.

Photo Import (full-size color iPods before the iPod classic). Full-size color iPods produced before the iPod classic can import photos from many digital cameras, using Apple's $29 iPod Camera Connector. When you connect a supported camera to your iPod using this device, the Photo Import command appears in the Photos screen. Click it, and you'll find a list of all the rolls (import sessions) for photos you've brought into the iPod. The iPod classic and 3G iPod nano are not compatible with this accessory.

Podcasts (click-wheel iPods only)

As you learn later in the book, *podcasts* are Internet broadcasts that you download and place on your iPod for later listening. Podcasts downloaded through the iTunes Store are routed to your iPod and placed under this entry on click-wheel iPods (**Figure 3.25**). On earlier iPods, you'll find the Podcasts entry in the Playlists screen.

Figure 3.25
Podcasts screen.

Extras

The Extras screen is the means to all the iPod's nonmusical functions—its contacts, calendars, clock, and games. Here's what you'll find for each entry.

Clocks

Yes, the iPod can tell time. Clicking Clocks displays the current time and date on today's traditional iPods. The Clocks screen displays both an analog and digital clock in the top part of the screen (**FIGURE 3.26**).

Figure 3.26
Clocks screen.

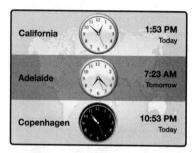

You can add clocks or edit the selected clock by pressing the Center button. When you do, a small bar appears that includes the words *Add, Edit,* and *Delete* (when you've added a clock), with Add selected by default. Press the Center button again, and a Region screen appears. Choose a region with the scroll wheel, press the Center button, and choose a city in the resulting City screen to create a clock that reflects the time in that city.

When you choose Edit, you're taken to that same Regions screen, where you can choose a region and then a city. Choosing Delete removes the selected clock. (If you have just one clock on the screen, though, it can't be removed.)

Calendars

I also address calendar creation later in the book, so for now, just know that when you click the Calendars entry on one of today's traditional iPods, you'll see, at the very least, an All Calendars entry, To Do's, and Alarms. If you've created multiple calendars in an application such as Apple's iCal, you see separate calendar entries if you've asked iTunes to sync individual calendars (more on this in Chapter 7).

When you select All Calendars and press the Center button, the current month is displayed in a window with the current day highlighted (**Figure 3.27**). If a day has an event attached to it, that day displays a small red flag on the 5G iPod, iPod classic, and all iPod nanos. (Earlier iPods display events as small black rectangles.) The 3G iPod nano and iPod classic place small bell icons on days that include an alarm.

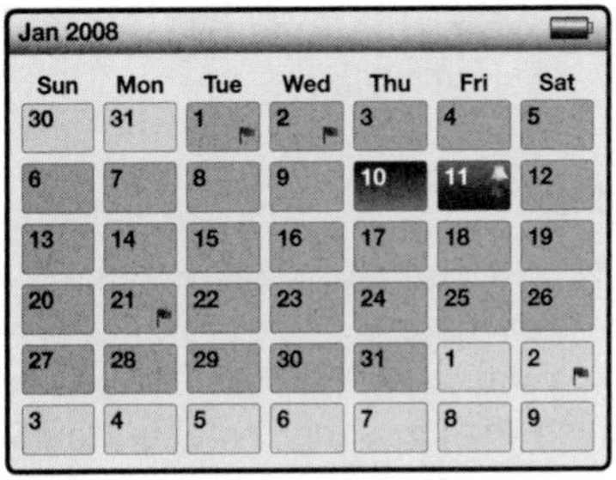

Figure 3.27
Calendars
screen.

Use the scroll wheel to move to a different day; scroll forward to look into the future; and scroll back to be transported back in time. To jump to the next or previous month, use the Next or Previous button, respectively. When you want to see the details of an event, scroll to its day and press the Center button. Any events scheduled for that day will appear in the resulting screen. Select an event and press the Center button, and you'll see any details attached to the event—the date, time, location, and any notes you've added, for example.

The To Do's entry is for any To Do items you've created in your computer's calendar application. A To Do's screen will give you a summary of the To Do (Finish the Book!, for example); its priority (hot items are given a priority of 1); and a due date, if you've created one. Notes are not included.

Finally, selecting Alarms and pressing the Center button cycles the options through Off, Beep, and None. Off means the iPod won't alert you to alarms. Beep indicates that the iPod will produce an audible beep. Setting the iPod to None activates a visual alert but no audible alarm.

Contacts

I also discuss how to create contacts in Chapter 7. In the meantime, you need to know only that to access your contacts, you choose Contacts in the Extras screen and press the Center button. Scroll through your list of contacts and press the button again to view the information within a contact. If a contact contains more information than will fit in the display, use the scroll wheel to scroll down the window.

If you haven't placed any contacts on your 3G iPod nano or iPod classic, when you select Contacts in the Extras screen, the right side of the display reads *No Contacts*. If you press the Center button at this point, nothing happens.

On earlier iPods, clicking the Contacts entry with no contacts on the iPod will reveal two entries in the Contacts screen: Instructions and Sample. You can probably guess that selecting Instructions provides directions on how to move contacts to your iPod. The Sample command shows you what a complete contact looks like.

Alarms

When you select Alarms and press the Center button, you'll see the Alarms screen, which has at least two entries: Create Alarm and Sleep Timer. If you've created any events in your computer's calendar program that have alarms attached to them, those events appear in this screen as well.

To create a new alarm, select Create Alarm and press the Center button. In the resulting screen, you'll see the option to turn the alarm on or off, as well as entries for Date, Time, Repeat, Sound, Label, and Delete.

Select Date and press the Center button, and the Alarms screen appears. You can enter dates by using the scroll wheel to scroll through the month, day, and year fields and the Next and Previous buttons to move from one field to the next. The Time entry works very much the same way.

Repeat allows you to choose how often the alarm occurs. You can select Once, Every Day, Weekdays, Weekends, Every Week, Every Month, or Every Year.

Sounds lets you choose Tones (None, which displays just a visual alarm, or Beep, which displays that visual alarm *and* causes the iPod to beep) or Playlists. When you choose Playlists and press the Center button, you can choose a playlist to play when the alarm goes off. This option is useful if your iPod is plugged into a speaker system or an iPod-compatible alarm clock.

A Label feature that appears for the first time on today's traditional iPods lets you choose one of 23 labels for your alarm, including Wake Up, Work, Party, Anniversary, and Take Medicine.

Finally, you can undo the alarm you're creating by scrolling down to Delete and pressing the Center button.

When an alarm goes off, a visual alarm appears that details the alarm—the time, date, and label. In this screen, you can choose to dismiss the alarm or snooze.

The Sleep Timer entry in the Alarms screen is for all those who like to fall asleep to music. Just plug your iPod into a speaker system (or wear headphones, I suppose, if you don't mind sleeping with them on), start it playing, and set a sleep timer (Off or 15, 30, 60, 90, or 120 minutes). The iPod will play for the time indicated; then it, too, will go to sleep.

Games

The 3G iPod nano and iPod classic include three games: iQuiz, Klondike, and Vortex. To play one of them, just select Games, press the Center button, select the game, and press that button once again. The games work this way:

iQuiz. As its name implies, iQuiz is a quiz-show kind of game. By default, you have a choice of four quizzes: Music Quiz 2, Movie Trivia, Music Trivia, and TV Show Trivia. Music Quiz 2 uses music stored on your iPod as the basis for its questions (**FIGURE 3.28**). It may play a tune, for example, and ask you whether such-and-such a title is correct. Answer yes or no by using the scroll wheel and Center button. Movie Trivia, Music Trivia, and TV Show Trivia use prepackaged questions and answers contained on the iPod. For all questions, you have about 15 seconds to answer.

 tip You can create your own games for iQuiz. Apple tells you how at www.apple.com/itunes/store/games/iquiz.html.

Figure 3.28
iQuiz game.

Klondike. Klondike is the classic solitaire game (**Figure 3.29**). To play, arrange alternating colors of cards in descending sequence—a sequence that could run jack of hearts, 10 of spades, 9 of diamonds, 8 of clubs, and so on—in the bottom portion of the screen. In the top portion of the window, you arrange cards in an ascending sequence of the same suit—ace, 2, 3, 4, and 5 of hearts, for example.

Figure 3.29
Klondike game.

Navigating this game is not completely intuitive. Use the scroll wheel to move the hand pointer to the card you want to move. Press the Center button to move the selected card to the bottom of the screen. Then move the pointer to where you want to place the card and press Center again. The game tries to be helpful by moving the pointer to the place where you're most likely to place the card.

Vortex. This game is a bit like the classic arcade game Breakout (or Brick), in which you bounce a ball off a wall to break down a barrier (**Figure 3.30**). In this case, the wall is round, and your paddle rotates around the outside of the wall. Press the Center button to unleash the ball and control the paddle with the scroll wheel.

Figure 3.30
Vortex game.

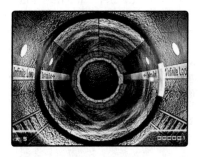

Notes

New with the 3G iPods is a Notes feature that allows you to store text files (up to 4 KB, or 4,096 characters) on your iPod. To add notes to your iPod, mount the iPod on your computer (the iPod must be configured to appear on the desktop), double-click the iPod to reveal its contents, and drag a text file into the iPod's Notes folder. When you unmount your iPod, you'll find the name of your text file in the Notes area of the Extras screen. The 1G and 2G iPods don't have this function.

Screen Lock

Screen Lock is a feature for...well, locking your iPod's screen. Like a cheap bike lock, this lock lets you create a four-digit password using numbers from 0 through 9. The interface on the 5G iPod and the 1G and 2G nanos features a round combination wheel with four digits above it. The 3G nano and iPod classic place the four digits in a row (**FIGURE 3.31**). To move from one digit to another, use the Next and Previous buttons. Pressing the Center button also takes you to the next digit and, when you reach the final digit, sets the code. You'll be asked to confirm the combination by entering it again. A lock icon will appear when the iPod is locked. To unlock it, press the Center button and enter the combination when prompted.

Figure 3.31
Screen Lock.

Stopwatch

The Stopwatch tracks total time and lap time. Choose Stopwatch and click the Center button to be taken to the Stopwatch screen. The first time you use the stopwatch on a 3G iPod nano or iPod classic, you'll see a picture of a stopwatch with a Play/Pause button next to it. Press the Center button to start the timer (**FIGURE 3.32**).

Each time you press the Center button as the timer runs, a lap time is added to the screen, as well as to a timer log. (The screen can display up to three lap times along with the current timer.) To pause the stopwatch, just press the Play/Pause button. You can keep the timer running by pressing the Menu button.

Figure 3.32
Stopwatch.

When you press that Menu button, the Stopwatch screen splits so that the stopwatch is on the right and a list of commands is on the left. This list includes Resume, which takes you back to the full-screen view of the timer; New Timer, for creating a new timer and saving the previous timer to the timer log; Clear Logs, which deletes any logs saved on the iPod; Current Log, which shows you the statistics for the current log (including date, time, and the shortest, longest, and average lap times); and then a list of any logs you've saved. Similar to the Current Log, these logs include date, time, and lap data.

Nike + iPod (iPod nano only)

This command appears only if you've plugged the Nike + Sport Kit receiver into your iPod nano's Dock Connector port. It leads to a Workout screen that allows you to choose among four main options: Basic, Time, Distance, and Calories. Within a Settings screen, you'll also find menu options for PowerSong (one track you've chosen that will activate with the press of the Center button at a key point of your workout); Spoken Feedback (choose either a male or a female voice to issue feedback); Distances (miles or kilometers); and Sensor, where you calibrate the Sport Kit for your body.

Voice Memos

Late-model full-size iPods and the 2G and 3G iPod nano can record voice memos with a compatible microphone adapter. When you plug such an adapter into the Dock Connector port, the Voice Memos command appears in the 3G iPod nano's and iPod classic's main screen (it appears in the Extras screen on earlier iPods). Currently, only three devices—Belkin's TuneTalk Stereo, Griffin Technology's iTalk Pro, and XtremeMac's MicroMemo—are compatible with today's iPods.

Click the Center button, and you're taken to the Voice Memos screen, where you can choose to record a new voice memo or play back memos you've already recorded. When you sync your iPod with iTunes, your recordings are transferred to a Voice Memos playlist in iTunes' source list. During the process, the memos are removed from the iPod.

Settings

The Settings screen (**FIGURE 3.33**) is the path to your iPod preferences—including backlight timer and startup-volume settings, EQ selection, and the language the iPod displays. The following sections look at these settings individually.

Figure 3.33
iPod Settings.

About

With the latest batch of iPods, Apple completely refreshed the look of the About screen and did so in a very helpful way. When you select About, the right side of the display tells you the name of your iPod, as well as how much free space remains on it (refer to Figure 3.33). Press the center button once, and you see a graphic display similar to iTunes' Capacity bar that provides details about the iPod's storage and how it's being used. Here, you'll learn how much space has been used and how much remains, as well as get a general notion of how much of your storage is devoted to audio, video, photos, and data.

For a much more specific idea of what's on your iPod, press the Center button again. In the next screen, you'll see exactly how many songs, videos, podcasts, photos, games, and contacts your iPod holds. Press the Center button one more time, and you'll see your iPod's serial number, model number, and software version.

Shuffle

Selecting Shuffle and pressing the Center button rotates you through three settings: Off, Songs, and Albums. When Shuffle is set to Off, the iPod plays the songs in a playlist in the order in which they appear onscreen. The Songs setting plays all the songs within a selected playlist or album in random order. If no album or playlist is selected, the iPod plays all the songs on the iPod in random order. And the Albums setting plays the songs within each album in order but shuffles the order in which the albums are played.

Repeat

The Repeat setting also offers three options: Off, One, and All. When you choose Off, the iPod won't repeat songs. Choose One, and you'll hear the selected song play repeatedly. Choose All, and all the songs within the selected playlist or album will repeat when the playlist or album has played all the way through. If you haven't selected a playlist or album, all the songs on the iPod will repeat after they've played through.

Main Menu

The Main Menu command offers you a way to customize what you see in the iPod's main screen. Choose Main Menu, and press the Center button. In the resulting screen, you can choose to view a host of commands. To enable or disable a command, press the Center button to toggle the command on or off. To return the main menu to its default setting, choose the Reset Menu command, press the Center button, choose Reset in the Reset Menus screen, and press the button again.

Music Menu

New to the 3G iPod nano and iPod classic, this menu works just like the Main Menu command. The difference is that the commands in this screen apply to the Music menu. This command also includes a Reset Menu entry.

Volume Limit

This feature was added in the middle of 2006 at the request of parents who were afraid their kids would blow out their ears by playing music at too high a volume. On display-bearing iPods, select Volume Limit and press the Center button, and you're taken to a screen where you can adjust the iPod's maximum volume up or down, using the scroll wheel and a typical iPod thermometer display. On the 3G iPod nano and iPod classic, press the Play/Pause button to set the limit. (On earlier iPods, you press the Center button to set the limit.) You're taken to a screen that offers you the option to set a combination for the volume limit—essentially letting you lock your kid's iPod volume to what you consider a safe and sane level.

To limit maximum volume on the iPod shuffle, connect it to your computer and select the shuffle in iTunes' Source list; in the Settings tab, enable the Limit Maximum Volume option. Drag the slider to the desired maximum volume. To demand a password, click the lock icon; then enter and verify a password in the resulting Volume Limit Password dialog box.

Backlight

The iPod's backlight pulls its power from the battery, and when backlighting is left on for very long, it significantly shortens the time you can play your iPod on a single charge. For this reason, Apple includes a timer that automatically switches off backlighting after a certain user-configurable interval. You set that interval by choosing the Backlight setting (called Backlight Timer on earlier iPods).

On iPods before the color iPods, the settings available to you are Off, 2 Seconds, 5 Seconds, 10 Seconds, 20 Seconds, 30 seconds, and (for those who give not a whit about battery life or who are running the iPod from the Apple Power Adapter) Always On.

Brightness

Today's traditional display-bearing iPods (and 5G iPods) carry a brightness setting. Select it and press the Center button, and you can dial your iPod's brightness up or down.

Audiobooks

One of the unique features of the click-wheel iPods is their ability to slow down or speed up the playback of audiobooks without changing the pitch of the narrator. When you select Audiobooks in the Settings screen, you're offered three options in the resulting Audiobooks screen: Slower, Normal, and Faster. The Slower and Faster commands slow or speed playback by about 25 percent, respectively.

You're likely thinking that it would take a minor miracle to pull this trick off without making the book sound odd. You're right; it would. And so far, Apple has failed to achieve this miracle. When you slow down an audiobook, the resulting audio sounds like it was recorded in a particularly reverberant bathroom; you hear a very short echo after each word. Files that are speeded up appear to have lost all the spaces between words, making the book sound as though it's being read by an overcaffeinated auctioneer.

EQ

In Chapter 2, devoted to the iPod touch, I describe what EQ does and what EQ settings that iPod offers. The traditional iPods offer these same EQ settings and work the same way as they do on the touch (**Figure 3.34**).

Figure 3.34
EQ.

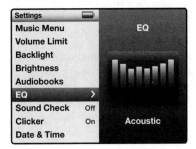

Sound Check

I mention Sound Check in Chapter 2 as well. Flip back for details.

Clicker

This option makes your iPod's click-wheel actually click—a handy option when you're scrolling through your iPod without looking at it. Clicker provides audible feedback when, for example, you're trying to move to the next command or playlist while driving. Recent click-wheel iPods allow you only to turn the clicker on and off. When the clicker is on, the click sound plays both through the headphones and through the iPod's tiny internal speaker.

Date & Time

The Date & Time command is your means of setting the time zone that your iPod inhabits, as well as the current date and time. In the Date & Time screen, you'll find these options:

Date. Click this command, and in the resulting screen, you'll see a numeric display of the date, including fields for month, date, and year. Move among these fields with the Next and Previous buttons, and increase or decrease their values with the scroll wheel. Press Menu when you're done.

Time. This screen is very similar to the Date screen. You use the scroll wheel to change the hour, minutes, AM/PM, date, month, and year values, and use the Forward and Previous buttons to move from value to value.

Time Zone. On the 3G nano and iPod classic, the Time Zone screen displays a map of the world. Use the scroll wheel to increment or decrement time. As you do, a red push-pin icon that represents the current time zone moves to the location of major cities within the current time zone.

Setting the time zone on a 5G iPod isn't nearly as much fun. The Time Zone screen on this iPod simply provides a list of major world cities. Select the one that represents your time zone and press the Menu button.

DST. The On/Off Daylight Savings Time command appears on the 3G iPod nano and iPod classic. This option isn't available on earlier iPods.

24 Hour Clock. If you're fond of military or international time (or if you just like saying "Fourteen hundred hours, sir!" in a commanding voice), this option is for you. It allows the iPod to keep time by using either a 12- or 24-hour clock.

Time in Title. This command allows the iPod to display the time in the iPod's title bar.

Sort By

The Sort By setting allows you to sort your contacts by last or first names.

Language

All display-bearing iPods since the 5G iPod can display 21 languages. Here's where you set which language your iPod will display.

Legal

If you care to view a few copyright notices, feel free to choose the Legal setting and press the Center button.

Reset Settings

As the name implies, selecting Reset Settings, using the scroll wheel to select Reset, and pressing the Center button will reset settings to their default. Your iPod's music will stay right where it is; this command just restores the interface to the way it was when the iPod came out of the box.

Shuffle Songs

One might think that choosing this option causes the iPod to play all the material on the iPod in random order. Not exactly. Shuffle Songs changes its behavior based on the Shuffle setting in the iPod's Settings screen. It works this way:

If you press Shuffle Songs when Shuffle is set to Off or to Songs, the iPod will play songs at random. (Note that it won't play any files it recognizes as audiobooks.)

If you press Shuffle Songs when Shuffle is set to Albums, the iPod picks an album at random and then plays the songs on that album in succession (the order in which they appear on the album). When that album finishes playing, the iPod plays a different album.

Note that if you also switch the Repeat command in the Settings menu to All and press Shuffle Songs, the iPod plays through all the songs on the iPod in the order determined by the Shuffle command and then repeats them in the same order in which they were shuffled originally. If you have three songs on your iPod—A, B, and C—and the iPod shuffles them to be in B, C, A order, when they repeat, they'll repeat as B, C, and A. The iPod won't reshuffle them.

Now Playing

When you select Now Playing, you'll see the name of the currently playing (or paused) track on the right side of the split-screen display. Press the Center button, and you're taken to the Now Playing screen.

4

iTunes and You

A high-performance automobile is little more than an interesting amalgam of metal and plastic if it's missing tires and fuel. Sure, given the proper slope (and, perhaps, a helpful tailwind), that car is capable of movement, but the resulting journey leaves much to be desired. So, too, the iPod is a less-capable music-making vehicle without Apple's multitrick media manager/player, iTunes. The two—like coffee and cream, dill and pickle, and Fred and Ginger— were simply meant for each other.

To best understand what makes the iPod's world turn, you must be familiar with how it and iTunes 7 work together to move music (and pictures and videos, in the case of some recent iPods) on and off your iPod. In the following pages, you'll learn just that.

Getting the Goods

You have three ways to get tunes into iTunes:

- Recording (or *ripping,* in today's terminology) an audio CD

- Importing music that doesn't come directly from a CD (such as an audio track you down-loaded or created in an audio application on your computer)

- Purchasing music from an online emporium such as Apple's iTunes Store

The following sections tell you how to use the first two methods. The iTunes Store (and its wireless partner, the iTunes Wi-Fi Music Store) is a special-enough place that I devote all of Chapter 5 to it.

Rip a CD

Apple intended the process of converting audio-CD music to computer data to be painless, and it is. Here's how to go about it:

1. Launch iTunes.

2. Insert an audio CD into your computer's CD or DVD drive.

By default, iTunes tries to identify the CD you've inserted. It logs on to the Web to download the CD's track information—a very handy feature for those who find typing such minutia to be tedious.

The CD appears in iTunes' Source list under the Devices heading, and the track info appears in the Song list to the right (**Figure 4.1**).

Figure 4.1
A selected CD and its tracks.

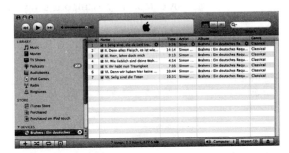

Then iTunes displays a dialog box, asking whether you'd like to import the tracks from the CD into your iTunes Library.

3. Click Yes, and iTunes imports the songs; click No, and it doesn't.

note You can change this behavior in iTunes' Preferences window. In the Importing tab of the Advanced pane, you find an On CD Insert pop-up menu. Make a choice from that menu to direct iTunes to show the CD, begin playing it, ask to import it (the default), import it without asking, or import it and then eject it.

Figure 4.2
iTunes' Import
CD button:
Let 'er rip.

4. If you decided earlier not to import the audio but want to do so now, simply select the CD in the Source list and click the Import CD button in the bottom-right section of the iTunes window (**Figure 4.2**).

iTunes begins encoding the files via the method chosen in the Importing tab of the Advanced pane of the iTunes Preferences window (**Figure 4.3**). By default, iTunes imports songs in "high quality" AAC format at 128 Kbps. (For more on encoding methods, see the sidebar "Import Business: File Formats and Bit Rates.")

Figure 4.3
iTunes'
Importing tab.

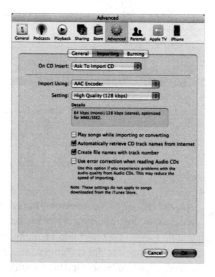

tip   To import only certain songs, uncheck the boxes next to the titles of songs you don't want to import; then click the Import CD button.

5. Click the Music entry in the Source list.

You'll find the songs you just imported somewhere in the list.

6. To listen to a song, click its name in the list and then click the Play icon or press the spacebar.

Import Business: File Formats and Bit Rates

MP3, MPEG-4, AAC, AIFF, WAV... is the computer industry incapable of speaking plain English?

It may seem so, given the plethora of acronyms floating through modern-day Technotopia. But the lingo and the basics behind it aren't terribly difficult to understand.

MP3, AAC, AIFF, and WAV are audio file formats. The compression methods used to create MP3 and AAC files are termed *lossy* because their encoders remove information from the source sound file to create these smaller files. Fortunately, these encoders are designed to remove the information you're least likely to miss—audio frequencies that humans can't hear easily, for example.

AIFF and WAV files are uncompressed, which means that they contain all the data in the source audio file. When a Macintosh pulls audio from an audio CD, it does so in AIFF format, which is the native uncompressed audio format used by Apple's QuickTime technology. WAV is an AIFF variant used extensively with the Windows operating system.

iTunes supports one other compression format: Apple Lossless. This format is termed a *lossless* encoder because it shrinks files by removing redundant data without discarding any portion of the audio spectrum. This scheme yields sound files with all the audio quality of the source files at around half their size.

continues on next page

Import Business: File Formats and Bit Rates *continued*

iTunes and the iPod also support the H.264 and MPEG-4 video formats. These, too, are compressed formats that allow you to fit a great big movie on a tiny iPod.

Now that you're familiar with these file formats, I'll touch on resolution as it applies to audio and video files.

You probably know that the more pixels per inch a digital photograph has, the crisper the image (and the larger the file). Resolution applies to audio as well. But audio defines resolution by the number of kilobits per second (Kbps) contained in an audio file. *With files encoded similarly*, the higher the kilobit rate, the better-sounding the file (and the larger the file).

I emphasize *with files encoded similarly* because the quality of the file depends a great deal on the encoder used to compress it. Many people claim that if you encode a file at 128 Kbps in both the MP3 and AAC formats, the AAC file will sound better.

The Import Using pop-up menu lets you choose to import files in AAC, AIFF, Apple Lossless, MP3, or WAV format. The Setting pop-up menu is where you choose the resolution of the AAC and MP3 files encoded by iTunes by choosing Custom from the menu. iTunes' default setting is High Quality (128 Kbps). To change this setting, choose Higher Quality (256 Kbps) or Custom from the Setting pop-up menu. (Spoken Podcast is another option when you choose the AAC Encoder, but it produces quality that's good only for spoken-word audio.) If you choose Custom, the AAC Encoder dialog box will appear. Choose a different setting—in a range from 16 Kbps to 320 Kbps—from the Stereo Bit Rate pop-up menu (**FIGURE 4.4**). Files encoded at a high bit rate sound better than those encoded at a low bit rate (such as 96 Kbps). But files encoded at higher bit rates also take up more space on your hard drive and iPod.

The preset options for MP3 importing include Good Quality (128 Kbps), High Quality (160 Kbps), and Higher Quality (192 Kbps). If you don't care to use one of these settings, choose Custom from this same pop-up menu. In the MP3 Encoder dialog box that appears, you have the option to choose a bit rate ranging from 8 Kbps to 320 Kbps.

Resolution is important for video as well. Fortunately (because an explanation beyond this gross simplification is beyond the scope of this slim volume), iTunes doesn't require or even allow you to muck with encoding video in any way, shape, or form. Movies are either encoded in such a way that they play on your iPod, or they aren't.

Figure 4.4

The Stereo Bit Rate pop-up menu.

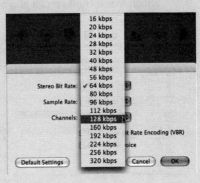

Move music into iTunes

Ripping CDs isn't the only way to put music files on your computer. Suppose that you've downloaded some audio files from the Web and want to put them in iTunes. You have three ways to do that:

• In iTunes, choose File > Add to Library.

When you choose this command, the Add To Library dialog box appears. Navigate to the file, folder, or volume you want to add to iTunes, and click Choose (**Figure 4.5**). iTunes determines which files it thinks it can play and adds them to the library.

Figure 4.5
Navigate to tracks you want to add to iTunes via the Add To Library dialog box.

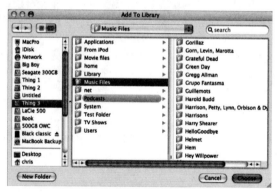

• Drag files, folders, or entire volumes to the iTunes icon in Mac OS X's Dock, the iTunes icon in Windows' Start menu (if you've pinned iTunes to this menu), or the iTunes icon in either operating system (at which point iTunes launches and adds the dragged files to its library).

- Drag files, folders, or entire volumes into iTunes' main window or the Library entry in the Source list.

In the Mac versions of iTunes, by default you'll find songs in the iTunes Music folder within the iTunes folder inside the Music folder inside your Mac OS X user folder. The path to my iTunes music files, for example, would be chris/Music/iTunes/iTunes Music.

Windows users will find their iTunes Music folder by following this path: *yourusername*/My Music/iTunes/iTunes Music.

You can use the same methods to add compatible videos and movies to your iTunes Library. Those videos will most likely appear in the Movies playlist in the Source list.

I say *most likely* because there are a few exceptions: Videos specifically designated as music videos appear in the Music playlist, and videos designated as TV shows appear in the TV Shows playlist. See the sidebar "Tag, You're It" at the end of this chapter for information on how to apply those video designations.

Creating and Configuring a Playlist

Before you put any media files (music or video) on your iPod, organize them in iTunes. Doing so will make it far easier to find the media you want, both on your computer and on your iPod. The best way to organize that material is through playlists.

A *playlist* is simply a set of tracks and/or videos that you believe should be grouped in a list. The organizing principle is completely up to you. You can organize songs by artist, by mood, by style, by song length... heck, if you like, you can have iTunes automatically gather all your 1950s polka tunes with the letter *z* in their titles. Similarly, you can organize your videos by criteria including director, actor, and TV-series title. You can mix videos and music tracks within playlists as well, combining, say, music videos and music tracks by the same artist. As far as playlists are concerned, you're the boss.

The following sections look at ways to create playlists.

Standard playlists

Standard playlists are those that you make by hand, selecting each of the media files you want grouped. To create a standard playlist in iTunes, follow these steps:

1. Click the large plus (+) icon in the bottom-left corner of the iTunes window, or choose File > New Playlist (Command-N on the Mac, Ctrl-N in Windows).

2. In the highlighted field that appears next to that new playlist in the Source list, type a name for your new playlist (**Figure 4.6**).

Figure 4.6
Enter a name
for your playlist.

3. Click an appropriate entry in the Source list—Music, Movies, TV Shows, or Podcasts—and select the tracks or videos you want to place in the playlist you created.

4. Drag the selected tracks or videos to the new playlist's icon.

5. Arrange the order of the tracks or videos in your new playlist.

   To do this, click the number column in the main window, and drag tracks up and down in the list. When the iPod is synchronized with iTunes, this order is how the songs will appear in the playlist on your iPod.

   If the songs in your playlist come from the same album, and you want the songs in the playlist to appear in the same order as they do on the original album, click the Album heading.

Playlist from selection

You can also create a new playlist from selected items by following these steps:

1. Command-click (Mac) or Ctrl-click (Windows) songs or videos to select the files you'd like to appear in the new playlist.

2. Choose File > New Playlist from Selection (Command-Shift-N on a Mac; the Windows version of iTunes has no keyboard shortcut).

   A new playlist containing the selected items will appear under the Playlists heading in the iTunes Source list. If all selected tracks are from the same album, the list will bear the name of the artist and album. If the tracks are from different albums by the same artist, the playlist will be named after the artist. If you've mixed tracks from different artists or combined music with videos, the new playlist will display the name *untitled playlist*.

3. To name (or rename) the playlist, type in the highlighted field.

Smart Playlists

Smart Playlists are slightly different beasts. They include tracks that meet certain conditions you've defined—for example, OutKast tracks encoded in AAC format that are shorter than 4 minutes. Here's how to work the magic of Smart Playlists:

1. In iTunes, choose File > New Smart Playlist (Command-Option-N on the Mac, Ctrl-Alt-N in Windows).

   You can also hold down the Option key on the Mac or the Shift key on a Windows PC and then click the gear icon that replaces the plus icon at the bottom of the iTunes window.

2. Choose your criteria.

   You'll spy a pop-up menu that allows you to select items by various criteria—including artist, composer, genre, podcast, bit rate, comment, date added, and last played—followed by a Contains field. To choose all songs by Elvis Presley and Elvis Costello, for example, you'd choose Artist from the pop-up menu and then enter **Elvis** in the Contains field.

   You can limit the selections that appear in the playlist by minutes, hours, megabytes, gigabytes, or number of songs. You may want the playlist to contain no more than 2 GB worth of songs and videos, for example.

   You'll also see a Live Updating option. When it's switched on, this option ensures that if you add any songs or videos to iTunes that meet the criteria you've set, those files will be added to the playlist. If you add a new Elvis Costello album to iTunes, for example, iTunes updates your Elvis Smart Playlist automatically.

3. Click OK.

   A new playlist that contains your smart selections appears in iTunes' Source list.

You don't have to settle for a single criterion. By clicking the plus icon next to a criterion field, you can add other conditions. You could create a playlist containing only songs you've never listened to by punk artists whose names contain the letter *J*.

Organize playlists in folders

You can also file playlists in folders. By invoking the File > New Folder command (Command-Option-Shift-N for the Mac and Ctrl-Shift-N in Windows), you can lump a bunch of playlists into a single folder. Folders are a great way to keep your playlists separate from your spouse's or to gather groups of similar playlists (All My Jazz Playlists, for example).

At one time, folders didn't translate to the iPod; however, the 3G iPod nano and the iPod classic do offer nested playlist hierarchies. The iPod touch doesn't. Instead, when you move a folder full of playlists into the iPod touch, all those playlists appear as separate entries in the touch's Playlists screen.

Move Music and Video to the iPod (shuffle Excluded)

note The next few pages don't apply to the iPod shuffle, as its iTunes interface is significantly different from the one used for other iPod models. Because it is so different, I've chosen to devote the latter portion of this chapter to the shuffle.

Now that your media is organized, it's time to put it on your 'pod. The conduit for moving music, podcasts, audiobooks, videos, and (for some iPods) games to the iPod is iTunes—which, fortunately, can be fairly flexible in the way it goes about the process.

You have several ways to configure iTunes so that your iPod is updated when you want it to be. It's just as possible to configure iTunes so that only the music and videos you want are copied to your iPod. The key is the iPod Preferences window.

To start, plug your iPod into your computer, and launch iTunes. (By default, iTunes launches when you connect the iPod.) The iPod appears under the Devices heading in iTunes' Source list (**Figure 4.7**). To open the iPod Preferences window, select the iPod in the Source list.

Figure 4.7
An iPod
in iTunes'
Source list.

Within the iPod Preferences window, you'll find eight panes if you have a 5G iPod, 3G iPod nano, or iPod classic: Summary, Music, Movies, TV Shows, Podcasts, Photos, Contacts, and Games. Those with an iPod touch will find seven panes: Summary, Music, Movies, TV Shows, Podcasts, Photos, and Info. If you have a color iPod that doesn't offer video (including 1G and 2G iPod nanos), the Movies, TV Shows, and Games tabs will be absent. For monochrome iPods, the Photos tab will also be missing.

Below these tabs, you'll see the Capacity bar (**Figure 4.8**), a thermometerlike display that details how much media is on your iPod. With any of today's display-bearing iPods plugged into your computer, you'll see entries for Audio, Video, Photos, Other (read: data like files you've copied to the iPod, notes, contacts, and calendars), and Free Space. Click the bar, and the display cycles through the amounts of storage used by each kind of media (measured in GB and MB); the numbers of items of each kind of media (7,660 songs, 109 videos, and 6,098 photos, for example); and how long it would take to play all the audio and video files (26.6 days, for example).

Figure 4.8
The Capacity bar.

Here's how the panes shake out.

Summary

In iTunes 7, the Summary pane provides such details about your iPod as its name, capacity, software version number, serial number, and format (Macintosh or Windows). It also tells you the version of the iPod software it's running and offers you the option to update that software if newer software is available or to restore your iPod (essentially, erase its contents and give it a new operating system). I cover the ins and outs of restoring your iPod in Chapter 9.

Finally, the Summary tab offers these options.

Open iTunes When This iPod Is Connected

Most likely, you're going to want to sync or otherwise muck with your iPod when you plug it into your computer. This option saves you the trouble of launching iTunes manually.

Sync Only Checked Songs and Videos

This option provides fine control over which files you sync to the iPod. Checking the box for this option lets you prevent files from loading onto the iPod by unchecking the small check boxes next to their names in playlists and Library lists.

 Care to check or uncheck all the songs in a playlist at the same time? On the Mac, hold down the Command key and click any check box in the playlist. In Windows, hold down the Control key and do the same thing. When you uncheck a box, all boxes will be unchecked; check a box, and all boxes will be checked.

Manually Manage Music and Videos

This small option offers a lot of power. To understand its usefulness, it's helpful to know that by default, when you sync iTunes and the iPod, iTunes moves only the files you ask it for onto the iPod and erases everything else from the device. This arrangement can be a real bother if you've moved your iPod from one computer to another, and the contents of the second computer don't match those of the first.

Managing files manually allows you to add music (and videos, for compatible iPods) to your iPod without erasing any other media. When you select this option, all the playlists on your iPod appear below the iPod's icon in the iTunes Source list. (For the sake of simplicity, I'll say that the Music, Movies, TV Shows, Podcasts, and Audiobooks entries count as playlists.)

To add media files to the iPod manually, just select them in one of iTunes' playlists, and drag them to the iPod's icon in the Source list or to one of the iPod's standard (not Smart) playlists (**Figure 4.9**). You can also drag files from your computer's desktop directly to the iPod, which copies the media to the iPod but not to your iTunes Library.

Figure 4.9
Moving music to the iPod manually.

Optionally, you can add songs by genre, artist, or album by using iTunes' browser. To do so, follow these steps:

1. In iTunes, choose View > Show Browser (Command-B in Mac OS X; Ctrl-B in Windows).

   A pane divided into Genre, Artist, and Album columns appears at the top of iTunes' main window.

2. Click an entry in one of the columns.

If you want to copy all the Kate Bush songs in your iTunes Library to the iPod, for example, click Ms. Bush's name in the Artist column. To copy all the reggae tunes to the iPod, select Reggae in the Genre column.

3. Drag the selected item to the iPod's icon in the Source list or to a playlist you've created on the iPod.

To remove songs from the iPod, select the songs you want to remove within the iPod entry in the Source list; then press your keyboard's Delete key (or Control-click on the Mac or right-click for Windows, and choose Clear from the contextual menu). Mac users can also drag the songs to the Trash.

tip **When you remove songs from your iPod, you don't remove them from your computer. Unless you select a song in iTunes' Library and delete it, the song is still on your hard drive.**

You can even copy entire playlists to other playlists by dragging one playlist icon on top of another. This method works for both iTunes and iPod playlists, though you can't drag a playlist on the iPod to an iTunes playlist and expect the songs to copy over. Under most circumstances, tracks on the iPod don't copy to your computer (unless you know the tricks detailed in Chapter 8).

But wait—there's more. iTunes 7 includes two new views: Album and Cover Flow view. Click the second button in the View palette at the top of the window to see Album view; Cover Flow view appears when you click the third button (**FIGURE 4.10**). As their names hint, these views let you see your music by album cover.

Figure 4.10
iTunes' View
buttons.

Specifically, in Album view, you'll see the artwork for any album available from the iTunes Store on the left side of the window and the contents of that album on the right side (**FIGURE 4.11**). Cover Flow view is kind of a lazy-Susan affair that represents your library as a series of covers (**FIGURE 4.12**). You can move music from these views to your iPod simply by dragging the cover art from the view to the iPod's icon. The contents of that album, video, or podcast will be transferred to the iPod.

Figure 4.11
Album view.

Figure 4.12
Cover Flow view.

note

When you choose to manage your songs and playlists manually, you'll be told that you have to disconnect all display-bearing iPods except the iPod touch manually—meaning that you have to take action to unmount the thing, rather than simply unplug it from your computer. To do so, you can click the Eject icon next to the iPod's name in the Source list, or select the iPod and then click the small icon of the iPod that appears in the bottom-right corner of the iTunes window. Alternatively, Mac users can switch to the Finder and drag the iPod to the Trash. When its icon disappears from the Desktop, you can unplug your iPod. Windows users can invoke the Safely Remove Hardware command from the system tray. If you unmount the iPod by doing something rash like unplugging it, your computer's operating system will complain, and your iPod may not have all the media you wanted it to have if it was busy doing something.

Enable Disk Use (all iPods except iPod touch)

The iPod is, at heart, an elegant storage device that happens to play music (and, in some cases, slide-shows and videos). You can mount all iPods except the iPod touch as a hard drive on your computer by enabling this option. When the iPod is mounted, you can use it just like a hard drive; copy files to it as you desire.

Music

The Music pane (**Figure 4.13**) contains options for syncing music and music videos to your iPod, as well as for displaying album artwork on all color iPods save for the iPod touch. (The iPod touch always syncs album artwork, so you won't find this option in the Music pane when you connect a touch.)

Figure 4.13

The Music pane.

Enabling the Sync Music option tells iTunes that you'd like it to sync its music collection to the iPod automatically. If you've enabled the Manually Manage Music and Videos option in the Summary pane, enabling the Sync Music option overrides the Manual option (iTunes will ask you if you're sure you want to do this). When you've chosen Sync Music, you then have the choice to sync all songs and playlists or just selected playlists.

Any songs currently on the iPod that aren't in the iTunes Library or in the selected playlists are erased from the iPod.

Why choose selected playlists rather than your entire music library? For one thing, your iPod may not have the capacity to hold your entire music collection. This option is also a good one to use when several members of your family share an iPod. It allows you to chunk up a music collection into multiple playlists and then rotate those playlists in and out of the iPod.

If you've removed songs from the iTunes Library and want them to remain on your iPod after the update, you'll want to avoid this option and manage your music manually.

Movies

The Movies pane (**FIGURE 4.14**) is similar to the Music pane. Here, you'll find the option to Sync Movies and then choices to sync All Movies, 1, 3, 5, or 10 Most Recent Unwatched Movies, or Selected Movies or Selected Playlists. iTunes provides this greater level of sync control because movies take up a lot of space, and a large movie collection and even the highest-capacity iPod may not mix.

Figure 4.14
The Movies pane.

Again, if you enable the Sync Movies option, you undo the Manually Manage Movies and Videos setting if you've switched it on.

TV Shows

The TV Shows pane (**FIGURE 4.15**) also provides greater flexibility than does the Music pane. Here, you can choose to sync all TV shows; 1, 3, 5, or 10 of the most recent; all unwatched TV shows; 1, 3, 5, or 10 of the most recent unwatched TV shows; or the selected TV shows or playlists.

Figure 4.15
The TV Shows pane.

Echoing my past statements, if you allow syncing of your TV shows, you disable the Manually Manage Movies and Videos setting.

Podcasts

It would be pretty silly to own a music player called
the iPod that didn't play podcasts. Yours does, and
this pane determines how podcasts are treated by
iTunes and the iPod (**Figure 4.16**).

Figure 4.16
The Podcasts
pane.

Much like with the TV Shows pane, you can choose
to sync all episodes of all podcasts; 1, 3, 5, or 10 most
recent of all your subscribed podcasts; all unplayed
podcasts you subscribe to; 1, 3, 5, or 10 of the most
recent unplayed episodes of all your podcasts; or
all new or 1, 3, 5, or 10 most recent new podcasts.
Alternatively, you can use these same options with
selected podcasts rather than all your subscribed
podcasts.

Photos (color iPods only)

If you have a color iPod, you can synchronize pictures between your photo library and your iPod. The key to doing so is within the Photos pane of the iPod Preferences window.

Sync Photos From option

When you enable this option, you'll see an alert that asks whether you're really sure you want to enable photo support. iTunes does this to warn you that any photos currently on the iPod will be replaced. You don't have the option to manage photos manually; thus, you have to be more careful about accidentally erasing pictures when you plug your color iPod into another computer.

With this option enabled, you can choose a source for your photos. On a Macintosh, you'll see iPhoto (and/or Aperture, if you've installed this Apple photo-editing application) listed in the Sync Photos From pop-up menu (**FIGURE 4.17**); you also have the option to choose images from the Pictures folder in your user folder or to select any other folder. This works pretty much as you'd expect.

When you choose iPhoto or Aperture, the option below the pop-up menu reads All Photos and Albums. When you enable this option, all the pictures in your iPhoto or Aperture library will be converted and copied to the iPod. You also have the option Selected Albums, which works much like the Selected Playlists option in the Music pane. Regardless of which option you choose, whenever you add new images to a selected album, the iPod automatically updates its photo library when it next synchronizes.

Figure 4.17
The Photos
pane.

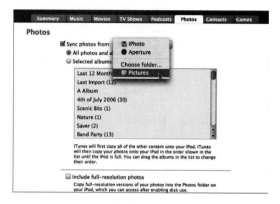

If you choose Pictures from this pop-up menu, the options below it change to All Photos and Albums and Selected Folders. The principles of iPhoto/Aperture import apply here as well. If you choose All Photos, iTunes rummages around in this folder and looks for compatible graphics files. If you choose Selected Folders, you can direct iTunes to look in only those folders that you select.

Finally, you can select Choose Folder. When you do, up pops a Change Photos Folder Location navigation window. Just traipse to the folder you want to pull pictures from, and click Choose. When you do this, the folder you've chosen replaces Pictures in the pop-up menu.

tip This method is a good way to copy every picture from your hard drive to your iPod. As far as iTunes is concerned, your hard drive is just another folder. Select it as the source folder with the All Photos option selected, and iTunes grabs all the compatible graphics files it can find, converts them, and plunks them onto your iPod.

This process is no more complicated for Windows users. The main difference is that the Windows version of iTunes offers no iPhoto option (and because no version of iPhoto is available for Windows, that's probably a good thing). Instead, you'll see the option to sync All or Selected Folders from your My Pictures folder or another folder of your choosing.

If you've installed Adobe Photoshop Elements (version 3 or later) or Adobe Photoshop Album on your PC, the Sync Photos From pop-up menu also contains entries for these programs, allowing you to import pictures from the albums that these programs create.

The tip I propose for copying all the pictures from your Mac to your iPod works with Windows as well. In this case, choose your C drive as the source. When you do, every compatible graphics file will be converted and copied.

Include Full-Resolution Photos (all color iPods except iPod touch)

Near the bottom of the Photos pane, you'll see the Include Full-Resolution Photos option, followed by this text:

Copy full-resolution versions of your photos into the Photos folder on your iPod, which you can access after enabling disk use.

This hunk of text is useful, in that it hints at where your full-resolution images are stored, but if space permitted, it would be even more useful if it continued with these words:

Oh, and don't get your hopes up, thinking that just because you've copied these full-resolution images to your iPod, you'll be able to view these exact images on your iPod or project them on a television. No, sir (or madam, as the case may be), this option is provided only as a convenient way to transfer your images to the iPod so that you can later attach it to a different computer and copy your pictures from here to there.

note **The Full Resolution folder, which appears within the iPod's Photos folder, is organized in a logical way. When you open the Full Resolution folder, you'll see a folder that bears the year the pictures were created. Within this folder are folders marked with the month of creation. Within one of these folders is a folder denoting the day of conception. So the folder hierarchy might look like this: Photos/Full Resolution/2008/2/28/ yourphotos.**

Contacts (all display-bearing iPods except iPod touch)

iTunes handles synchronization of contacts and calendars between your computer and iPod. The Contacts pane offers synchronization options for your computer's main contacts and calendars applications. From the Contacts pane on a Macintosh, you can choose to synchronize all your Apple Address Book contacts or just those contacts from selected groups. On a Windows PC, iTunes synchronizes Windows' Address Book or Microsoft Outlook contacts in the same way—either all contacts or selected groups of contacts. Only in the Macintosh version of iTunes do you also have the option to include the photo associated with your contact.

Below the Contacts section of the pane, you'll spy the Calendars section, which works similarly to Contacts. On a Mac, you can sync all your iCal calendars or just selected calendars. On a Windows PC, you have these same options for Microsoft Outlook calendars.

Games (5G iPod, 3G iPod nano, and iPod classic only)

The iTunes Store sells games made specifically for the iPod. Currently, The Store sells a small collection of games that are compatible with the 3G iPod nano, iPod classic, and 5G iPod. Buy one of these games, and you can play it on any (or all) of these iPod models. The Store also sells a larger collection of games designed specifically for the 5G iPod.

The Games pane is where you choose which games to sync to your iPod. Your choices are all games or selected games (chosen from a list of purchased games below). The iPod touch currently doesn't support games purchased from the iTunes Store.

Info (iPod touch only)

The iPod touch's Info pane is similar to the Contacts pane that appears for other iPods (**Figure 4.18**). It has some important differences, however.

Figure 4.18

The iPod touch's Info pane.

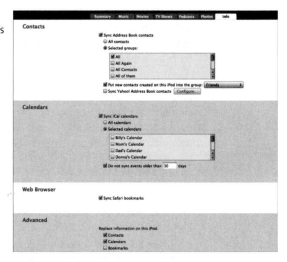

The first difference reflects the iPod touch's ability to create contacts on the iPod rather than just syncing them from an address-book application on your computer. At the bottom of the Contacts area, you'll find the option Put New Contacts Created on This iPod into the Group *X*, where *X* is a pop-up menu that lists the groups you've created in your computer's address book.

In the Macintosh version of iTunes, below this option, you'll find the Sync Yahoo! Address Book Contacts option. (The Windows version of iTunes puts this option in a pop-up menu within the Contacts area.) Enable this option, click the Configure button, and then click the Agree button in the resulting window, and you grant iTunes the right to access your Yahoo account for the purpose of synchronizing your contacts with your Yahoo address book.

The Calendars section is slightly different as well; it includes the Do Not Sync Events Older Than X Days option. Your iPod touch has limited storage, and there's no reason to fill it with old calendar events.

Below the Calendars area are two additional areas: Web Browser and Advanced. The Web Browser area simply offers you the option to sync your Safari bookmarks or, if you're running iTunes under Windows, your Internet Explorer bookmarks for use in the touch's version of the Safari Web browser (which I discuss in detail in Chapter 6).

Advanced includes options for replacing contact, calendar, and bookmark information on the iPod. These options are useful for those times when you plug your iPod touch into a different computer and want to sync or merge that computer's contacts, calendars, or bookmarks with your iPod.

Move Music to the iPod shuffle

As I mention earlier in the chapter, the iPod shuffle interacts differently with iTunes than a display-bearing iPod does. To begin with, because the shuffle lacks a screen, it doesn't need to offer options for synchronizing photos, videos, contacts, and calendars. The lack of a screen also means that you can do little to navigate a shuffle's music library. You are, in a very real sense, flying blind.

And then there's the shuffle's limited storage space. Because the current shuffles hold just 1 GB (and a previous model held only 512 MB), you don't have a lot of extra room for storing large music files. iTunes does its best to keep such files from being placed on your music player automatically.

With these limitations in mind, let's take a look at just what iTunes offers for the shuffle owner.

When you attach an iPod shuffle to your Mac or PC, by default, iTunes launches. When it does, the shuffle appears in the iTunes Source list under the Devices heading, just like any other iPod (save for the fact that its icon looks like a shuffle rather than a full-size iPod). Select that shuffle, and iTunes' main window shows two tabs: Settings and Contents, with the Contents tab front and center.

Contents tab

In the top part of the window, you see a list of the tracks you've loaded on the shuffle. At the bottom of the window, you see the Autofill pane (**FIGURE 4.19**), which contains the items described in the following sections.

Autofill button

Figure 4.19
The shuffle's
Autofill pane.

In theory, putting music on your shuffle is very simple. By default, iTunes is set up so that when you click the Autofill button, iTunes grabs a collection of random tracks from your iTunes Library and copies those tracks to your shuffle. But things don't have to work that way. Although the Autofill button, in league with the Autofill From pop-up menu (which you'll hear about in just a sec), is a powerful way to move music to your shuffle, you need never touch it.

Blasphemy? Perhaps. But the only way to ensure that you get *exactly* the music you want on your shuffle is to lay off this button. Instead, if your shuffle has anything on it, select it, select all its contents, and press your computer's Delete key. Then drag just the music you want from your iTunes Library onto the shuffle's icon.

To see the order in which songs will play if the shuffle is set to play from beginning to end, click the number heading in iTunes' main window. To save that playlist so that you don't lose it when you later fill your shuffle with other music, select everything in the playlist, and choose File > New Playlist from Selection. A new playlist will be created in iTunes' Source list that includes all the selected tracks.

If you choose to bang the Autofill button, of course, it will do exactly what it says: fill your shuffle with as much as it can of the playlist selected in the Autofill From pop-up menu.

Autofill From pop-up menu

One way to customize your shuffle's contents more carefully is to feed it from specific playlists. You might create sets of music that make sense for particular activities—music for your next workout or for a car trip, for example. When you've created these playlists, you can choose the one you like from the Autofill From pop-up menu.

Choose Items Randomly

The shuffle was designed with random play in mind, but you can make it load specific tracks in a specific order by disabling this option. When you do, iTunes will take the playlist selected in the Autofill From pop-up menu and place as much of it as can fit, in order, on the shuffle. When you've flipped your shuffle into "play from beginning to end" mode, the playlist you load will play in that order. This technique is one way to ensure that the songs in an album you place on the shuffle play in the same order as they do on the album.

Choose Higher Rated Items More Often

I mean, honestly, what's the use of putting music or podcasts that you loathe on your shuffle? If you haven't thought of a good reason for rating your audio files, now you have one. Assign a rating of four or five stars to your favorite tracks, and those tracks are more likely to be moved to your shuffle when this option is enabled.

Replace All Items When Autofilling

When this option is selected, iTunes will wipe out whatever music the shuffle currently holds and replace it with selections from the playlist selected in the Autofill From pop-up menu. Leaving this box checked is a good way to help ensure that you get a fresh crop of music the next time you listen to your shuffle. It's not such a good choice, however, if you want to keep some selections on the shuffle (podcasts, for example) and remove others.

Uncheck this option, and check Only Update Checked Songs in the Settings tab (which I'll get to very shortly), and you've got a whole lot more control. This way, you can uncheck all your podcasts (or other tracks you want to keep) on the shuffle and then click the Autofill button. The stuff you want to keep stays put and is surrounded by new material.

Settings tab

The other tab you see when selecting an iPod shuffle in the Source list provides settings for formatting the little devil and managing its relationship with iTunes. The Settings tab (**FIGURE 4.20**) includes the some of the same options you find in a display-bearing iPod's Summary pane.

Figure 4.20
The shuffle's
Settings tab.

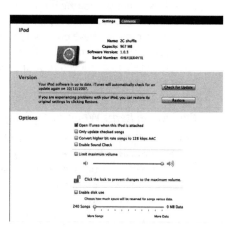

At the top of the pane, you'll find information regarding the shuffle's name, capacity, software version number, and serial number.

Below is the same Version area that you see for other iPods. Here, you can update or restore your iPod with the latest iPod software.

The Options area is where the good stuff happens. Here, you'll see options for launching iTunes when the shuffle is attached, updating only checked songs, converting higher-bit-rate songs to 128 Kbps AAC, enabling Sound Check, and enabling disk use. You're familiar with some of these options already. Let's look at the new ones.

Convert Higher Bit Rate Songs to 128 Kbps AAC

Although the shuffle can play uncompressed files (which you learned about earlier in the chapter), on a device with such limited storage, packing it with these large files isn't such a good idea. Enabling this option instructs iTunes to slim down stout files so that they take up less space on the shuffle.

iTunes won't automatically place Apple Lossless files on your shuffle; on the 1G shuffle, it also won't load AIFF files. If you drag such files to the shuffle to place them on the player manually, however, iTunes will automatically convert them to 128 Kbps AAC files when this option is enabled. Your files will remain in their original format on your computer, but compressed copies will be made just for the shuffle.

Enable Sound Check

Enable this option, and your shuffle will use those
Sound Check settings to play back tracks at a fairly
consistent volume.

Limit Maximum Volume

Enable the option, and adjust the slider to set a
maximum volume for the shuffle. Click the Lock icon
to password-protect this option.

Enable Disk Use

If you enable this option, you can mount the shuffle
on your computer and use it to store data files as
well as music files.

To help ensure that you've got some room left for
data files, iTunes includes a slider below this option
that allows you to determine how much of the
shuffle's storage space will be reserved for songs and
how much will go toward data storage. If you set the
slider to the halfway point on a 512 MB iPod shuffle,
you can fit approximately 60 4-minute 128 Kbps AAC
songs and 156 MB of data on your iPod. Double those
figures for a 1 GB shuffle.

Tag, You're It

So how does iTunes know about tracks, artists, albums, and genres? Through something called ID3 tags. *ID3 tags* are just little bits of data included in a song file that tell programs like iTunes something about the file—not just the track's name and the album it came from, but also the composer, the album track number, the year it was recorded, and whether it is part of a compilation.

These ID3 tags are the key to creating great Smart Playlists. To view this information, select a track, and choose File > Get Info. Click the Info tab in the resulting window, and you'll see fields for all kinds of things. You may find occasions when it's helpful to change the information in these fields. If you have two versions of the same song—perhaps one is a studio recording, and another is a live recording—you could change the title of the latter to include *(Live)*.

A really useful field to edit is the Comments field. Here, you can enter anything you like and then use that entry to sort your music. If a particular track would be great to fall asleep to, for example, enter **sleepy** in the Comments field. Do likewise with similar tracks, and when you're ready to hit the hay, create a Smart Playlist that includes "Comment is sleepy." With this technique under your belt, you can create playlists that fit particular moods or situations, such as a playlist that gets you pumped up during a workout.

5

The iTunes Store

In Chapter 4, you learned how to put the music and video you own on your iPod. Now it's time to look at a cool way to obtain new media. And by *cool*, I can mean nothing other than Apple's online digital media emporium: the iTunes Store. In the following pages, I take you on a tour of The Store and its untethered counterpart—the iTunes Wi-Fi Music Store—and show you the best ways to discover and purchase new media.

The One-Stop Shop

Apple has eschewed the typical Internet-commerce model of creating a Web site that users access through a Web browser. Although this model works reasonably well for countless merchants, it invariably requires customers to slog through Web page after Web page to find and pay for the items they desire. Apple wanted a service as immediate as the experience of going to a media megastore, gathering the music and movies you want, and taking them to the counter.

To replicate this experience, Apple placed The Store inside an application that was already built for music browsing (and, later, video browsing) and that many of its customers were likely to be familiar with: iTunes.

Having The Store incorporated into iTunes offers several benefits:

- **It's easy to access.** Just open iTunes and click the iTunes Store entry in the Source list. If your computer is connected to the Internet, the iTunes Store interface appears in the main iTunes window.

- **It's a cinch to find music, audiobooks, podcasts, music videos, TV shows, and movies.** First, enter a search term in the Search iTunes Store field, located in the top-right corner of the iTunes window. (This term can be pretty much anything you like: artist, album, song title, podcast title, TV show, movie, even a single word.) The latest version of iTunes will display a pop-up menu full of suggested items that match your query. You can select one of the suggestions or press the Mac's Return key or the PC's Enter key. In very little time, a window appears that's partitioned into categories containing items that match your query: Albums, Artists, Music Videos, TV Shows, Movies, Podcasts, and Audiobooks. If you type **Louie** in the search field, for example, you'll see links to a few albums (including *The Best of the Kingsmen*, due to their perennial frat-house favorite "Louie Louie"), as well as a music video by the artist Louie Louie and an audiobook by Louie Giglio.

At the top of the window, you'll see headings for All, Music, TV Shows, Music Videos, Audiobooks, Podcasts, and iTunesU (an area of The Store that holds educational material such as university lectures). Click one of these headings to narrow your search to just that category.

- **It's hard to get lost.** Should you ever wander into one of the scarier sections of The Store (say, the polka aisle), finding your way back to the main page is easy. Simply click the Home icon at the top of the iTunes window, and you're transported to the main page.

  Next to the Home icon, you'll see a path from your present location to the main page—Home/Music/World/Gigi/Gold & Wax, for example. To move up a level or two, simply click one of the entries in this hierarchy.

  Another way to retrace your steps is to use the Back and Forward buttons, just to the left of the

Home icon. These buttons are similar to the Back and Forward buttons in your Web browser. Click the Back button to move to the page you viewed previously. If you've backtracked and want to go forward again, click the Forward button.

- **It's tough to purchase media you don't want.** The Store allows you to sample a 30-second preview of every song, music video, and TV show it sells. Audiobooks get a 90-second preview. And movies offer the theatrical trailers you'd see in a theater. Highlight the item you want to preview; then click iTunes' Play button, Preview (audiobooks), or View Trailer (movies).

- **It couldn't be much easier to purchase media.** Simply create an Apple account, locate the media you want to buy, and click the Buy button next to the pertinent item. After iTunes confirms your decision to purchase, it downloads the item to your computer. Songs cost, on average, 99 cents apiece for the copy-protected version as well as for the iTunes Plus unprotected version (see "iTunes Plus" later in the chapter); albums vary but hover around $9.99; and music videos and TV shows, $1.99 each. Movies come in three prices. Library (read: older) movies are $9.99; preorders and movies released during the current week are $12.99; and current movies that are more than a week old are $14.99. Audiobooks can be priced from a little to a lot, and podcasts are free.

When the media is on your computer, you can copy it to your iPod (video plays only on 5G iPods, 3G iPod nanos, and iPod classics, of course), play it on up to five computers, and stream or copy it to the Apple TV set-top box. You can burn music to an audio CD that you can play anywhere you like. You can't burn any variety of video to a disc that can be played in a commercial DVD player. Instead, Apple allows you to burn music videos, TV shows, and movies as data for purposes of backup. (In other words, you're just copying the video files so that you can restore them to your computer if something should happen to the original.) You can do all this without leaving the iTunes application.

In short, the entire process is about as complicated as ordering and eating a Big Mac and fries (and a whole lot healthier!). Easy to use as it may be, however, The Store has hidden depths. In the following pages, I explain all that there is to know about The Store, and tell you how you and your iPod can put it to the best use.

Prepare to Shop

Ready to shop? Great. Let's make sure that you have the tools you need to get started. After you have those tools, I'll get you signed up with an account and then take you on an extensive tour of The Store.

What you need

Naturally, you need a Mac or a Windows PC and a copy of iTunes. Although it's not necessary to have an iPod to take advantage of The Store—media purchased at The Store can be played on your computer, and music can be burned to CD—the iPod technically is the only portable media player capable of playing protected music purchased at The Store.

Also, although you can access The Store via any Internet connection, you'll find it far more fun to shop with a broadband connection. A 4-minute protected song weighs in at around 4 MB. Such a download over a DSL or cable connection takes next to no time at all but can be terribly slow over a poky modem connection. And even with a DSL or cable connection, you could wait up to an hour to download a full-length movie from The Store.

As these pages go to print, The Store is available in 22 countries. Which store you're allowed to purchase media from depends on the issuing country of your credit card. If you have a credit card issued in Germany, for example, you can purchase media only from the German iTunes Store (though you don't physically have to be in Germany to do this—again, the credit card determines where you can shop).

Sign on

You're welcome to browse The Store the first time you fire up iTunes, but to purchase media, you must establish an account and sign in. Fortunately, Apple makes it pretty easy to do so. The process goes like this:

With your computer connected to the Internet, launch iTunes, and click the iTunes Store entry in iTunes' Source list; then click the Sign In button in the top-right corner of the iTunes window. If you have either an Apple ID and password or an AOL screen name and password, enter them and click the Sign In button; otherwise, click the Create Account button.

When creating an account, you'll need to enter a valid email address and create a password. After you've done these things, you'll enter some personal information so that Apple can identify you, if need be.

Finally, after you've traipsed through The Store's terms and conditions, you'll be asked for a credit-card number and your name, address, and phone number. Click Done and...well, you're done. You're now a member in good standing.

Navigate The Store's Floors

As I tap out these words, The Store carries more than 6 million songs, 100,000 podcasts, 30,000 audiobooks, 600 TV shows, 500 movies, and a trickle of iPod games. Fortunately, you needn't trudge through an alphabetical list of all these titles. Instead, Apple offers you multiple ways to browse its catalog of goodies. Let's look at The Store's floor plan and the best ways to navigate it.

The Store's main page offers a host of links for finding the media you desire (**Figure 5.1**). Much like a "real" media megastore, The Store places the day's most popular picks up front.

Figure 5.1
The Store's main page.

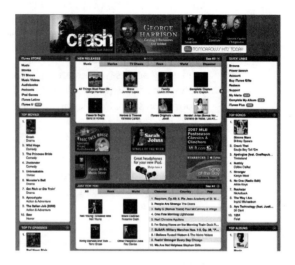

Across the top of the main page, you'll see a banner that changes from time to time. This banner may promote hot new singles or albums, exclusive tracks, music videos, TV shows, and movies.

Below the banner are tabbed, side-scrolling panes. The topmost pane offers tabs for new releases in the Music, Movies, and TV Shows categories, along with three additional music tabs (the genres of which can vary from time to time) to fill out the pane.

For those unfamiliar with these features, here's how the most significant music features shake out:

iTunes Collections. Clicking iTunes Collections takes you to something like a "greatest music hits of The Store" page. Here, you find links to best-selling iTunes Essentials collections (more on these in the next couple of pages); featured "The World Of" artist collections; and iTunes Live Sessions (live recordings sold exclusively at the iTunes Store).

iMix. iMix is your chance to inflict your musical values on the rest of the world by publishing a playlist of your favorite (or, heck, your least-favorite) songs. When you click the iMix link, you're taken to a page that contains three columns marked Top Rated, Most Recent, and Featured, all listing iMix playlists posted by fellow music lovers. Type a genre, artist name, or keyword (such as *summer* or *drive*) in the Search For field to narrow your choices, or just click an "album cover" to view the songs in an iMix (and buy them, if you like).

As enjoyable as it may be to view others' iMixes, creating your own is more fun. You can do so by following these steps:

1. Create a new playlist in iTunes, and give it a really cool name.

The cooler the name, the more likely others are to view your iMix.

2. Cruise through your iTunes Library, and drag into it songs you'd like to publish in an iMix.

note Your iMix can contain only songs available for purchase from The Store. If the iMix contains songs that are not available at The Store, those songs won't appear in the published playlist.

3. Round out your list with songs at The Store that you don't own.

An iMix doesn't require that you actually own the music you're recommending; you can drag previews of any song or audiobook from The Store into a playlist in iTunes' Source list. Feel free to add these previews to your iMix playlist.

4. Click the arrow to the right of your playlist's name.

When you click this arrow, a dialog box asks whether you'd like to give the playlist as a gift or publish it as an iMix.

5. Click Create iMix.

You'll be asked to sign in with your Apple ID. Then you'll be taken to The Store, and iTunes' main window will show you a picture of your iMix's album cover (a collage of album covers for the songs you've included).

6. Edit the title and description to suit your iMix.

7. Click Publish and then click Done.

Your iMix will be published to The Store and will remain there for 1 year. You'll receive an email confirmation of the iMix's publication and a link to it. Click the link, and iTunes takes you to your iMix's page. Here, you have the option to advertise your link to friends by clicking the Tell a Friend link.

Best Of The Store. A recent addition to the iTunes Store, Best Of The Store features weekly collections of cuts that are big news around iTunes. These collections lead off with the week's hot single and go on to feature more of the week's noteworthy releases.

iTunes Originals. iTunes Originals are albums created specifically for The Store by such artists as Jewel, New Order, The Flaming Lips, and Elvis Costello. These albums variously feature bonus cuts, live performances, and interviews in which the artists offer insights into the album's music tracks.

iTunes Essentials. Although you can purchase entire albums from The Store (and are occasionally required to purchase an entire album to get all the songs on it), it's mostly a song-based enterprise. By this, I mean that The Store encourages you to pick and choose just the pieces of music you like.

Given this idea, it makes sense that Apple would offer compilations of songs, organized by some catchy sort of theme—Women in Bluegrass, Animation Classics, or It Came from TV!, for example—or by an artist. Apple calls these compilations iTunes Essentials.

Yes, these are essentially Apple's own iMixes—
collections of songs the folks who work at The Store
think you'll like (**FIGURE 5.3**). Unlike most of The Store's
other albums, these compilations don't give you a
discount. If an iTunes Essential contains 25 songs,
you pay $24.75, or 99 cents per song.

Figure 5.3
iTunes
Essentials.

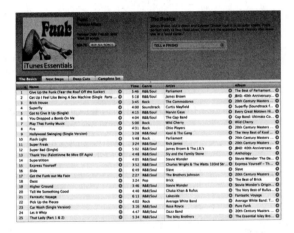

iTunes Essentials are offered in four configurations:
The Basics, Next Steps, Deep Cuts, and Complete Set.
As their names indicate, The Basics includes the most
obvious songs that fit a particular theme; Next Steps
offers slightly more obscure tracks; Deep Cuts hits
the fringes; and Complete Set offers all songs in the
previous three categories.

Celebrity Playlists. If you'd like to know what rocks the worlds of Sarah Silverman, Barry Zito, Jason Lee, and Poison (no, I'm not exactly sure which Poison pen picked this list), click these links. The resulting page offers a list of tunes an artist thinks worthy. You can preview and purchase songs—either individually or the entire list—directly from this page.

Just Added. To see lists of music added in the past 4 weeks, arranged by artist name, click this link.

Starbucks Entertainment. Apple has entered into partnership with Starbucks to sell music from Starbucks' music label—not just at The Store, but also through participating Starbucks outlets (more on this later in the chapter). This section of The Store is reserved for this music and for music that goes well with a double wet nonfat soy cappuccino.

Nike Sport Music. As mentioned earlier in the book, Nike and Apple have teamed to pair music and athletic shoes. This section of The Store features mixes designed for the perfect workout. Each mix includes an opening narration that describes the kind of workout the mix is for, followed by the songs.

iTunes Live from The Palms. Another co-marketing venture, this one involves offering live recordings of concerts performed at the Palms Resort in Las Vegas. Some concerts are audio only; others are videos.

Genres pane. Given all these links, as well as access to the Search and Browse functions, you should be well on your way, right? Perhaps. But don't leave the main Music page without checking out the Genre links. These tools are great to use when you're in the mood for a particular style of music. Just click a genre that appeals to you, such as Folk or Dance.

Choosing an item from the Genres pane takes you to a page devoted to that genre. This page is laid out similarly to the main Music page, containing at least a New Releases area and then other areas that are appropriate for that particular genre. Some genre pages include subcategory listings, whereas others call out subgenres within that genre—Vocals and Smooth Jazz on the Jazz page, for example.

The Today's Top Songs and Today's Top Albums lists change to reflect The Store's most popular songs and albums within that genre. On these pages, you'll also find links to the top 100 songs and top 100 albums for that genre.

Movies, TV Shows, and Music Videos

I lump these three categories together because the main pages for these media types offer the same kind of structure. Somewhere on each page, you'll see featured items, top sellers, new releases, and a categories breakdown—Comedy, Drama, and Kids & Family for movies, for example.

Audiobooks

This part of The Store resembles the Music section more than the sections that sell videos. Here, you'll find new releases, hot titles, staff favorites, category listings (Arts & Entertainment, Classics, Romance, and Sci Fi & Fantasy, for example), Popular Authors, and Top Shows and Periodicals (mostly audiobooks created from NPR's "This American Life" episodes).

Podcasts

The Store is a conduit for obtaining podcasts—those do-it-yourself, radiolike broadcasts that you've heard so much about. On the Podcasts page, you'll find a host of podcasts vying for your attention. The structure of the page changes so often that I'm not going to detail what you're likely to find here. Just know that you'll probably see a banner across the top that promotes podcasts deemed interesting by Apple; a Today's Top Podcasts list along the right side that lists that week's most popular 'casts; and a Categories sidebar on the left side that allows you to sort through podcasts by theme—Arts, Business, Comedy, and Technology, for example.

When you select a podcast, you'll be taken to a page devoted to it. From this page, you can download single episodes (by clicking the Get Episode button that appears to the right of the podcast) or subscribe to the podcast (by clicking the Subscribe button).

When you click Get Episode, iTunes switches to the Podcasts pane, where all your podcasts are listed, and begins downloading the podcast (**FIGURE 5.4**). You'll see a subject heading for the podcast—KCRW's Le Show, for example—and when you click the triangle next to that heading, you'll view a list of that program's individual shows.

Figure 5.4
The Podcasts pane.

Next to a show's subject heading, you'll spy a Subscribe button. When you click this Subscribe button or the Subscribe button in one of The Store's podcast pages, some previous episodes of the now-subscribed show will appear in the Podcasts pane, accompanied by a Get button that, when clicked, allows you to retrieve the shows. When new episodes become available, iTunes will download them automatically.

If you tire of receiving a particular show, just select its subject heading and click the Unsubscribe button at the bottom of the iTunes window. You'll no longer receive episodes.

iPod Games

What? You mean they're featuring hints on beating iQuiz, Klondike, and Vortex? No, thank heavens. iTunes 7 introduced iPod Games, which offers color games specifically designed for 5G iPods and now for 3G iPod nanos and iPod classics (**Figure 5.5**). All games—save iQuiz for the 5G iPod, which is 99 cents—are $4.99 apiece, and currently, very few of them are available for the 3G iPod nano and iPod classic. The 5G iPod has been supporting games longer, so more games are available for it.

Figure 5.5
An iPod game.

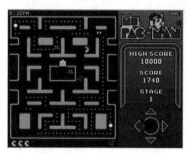

note Older games you've purchased for your 5G iPod are not compatible with the latest iPods.

Top of the Pops

Want to see lists of the hottest movies, TV shows, music videos, songs, albums, audiobooks, iPhone ringtones, and podcasts available from The Store? The Top boxes arrayed around the edges of The Store's main page offer just that. All these categories, save audiobooks and podcasts, list the day's top 10 items (audiobooks and podcasts list just the top five). If you care to view the top 100 items in a particular category, simply click the right-pointing arrow on the right side of each category heading.

Quick Links

The two links at the top of the list—Browse and Power Search—hint that there are more efficient ways to find music than clicking the titles you see on The Store's home page.

Browse

The Store offers a view much like the one you see in iTunes when you select a Library entry or a playlist and choose View > Show Browser. (In point of fact, choosing this command produces the same result as clicking the Browse link.) Click Browse, and iTunes' browser columns appear, listing Charts, Audiobooks, Movies, Music, Music Videos, Podcasts, and TV Shows.

Charts. Click Charts, and Chart appears in the second pane, listing Billboard Hot 100, Billboard Top Country, and Billboard Top R&B. Click one of these entries, and you can choose a year in the third pane. Select a year, and you'll see the top tracks for that year from that particular chart in the list below.

Audiobooks. Choose Audiobooks, and the next column adopts a Genre heading with various literary genres below (such as Classics, Kids & Young Adults, and Mystery). Choose a genre, and authors writing or speaking in that style appear in the Author/Narrator column to the right.

Movies. Select Movies, and a list of genres appears to the right—Action & Adventure, Comedy, and Thriller, for example. Choose one of these categories to see a list of movies that match.

Music. Clicking Music produces four additional columns: Genre, Subgenre, Artist, and Album. You know what to do.

Music Videos. Music Videos are broken into genres as well—Alternative, Blues, Holiday, Jazz, and Soundtrack, for example. Select a genre, and a list of appropriate artists appears to the right. Click an artist to see what he's or she's been up to in front of the cameras.

Podcasts. To the right of this entry, you see Category and Subcategory columns. Choose Technology, for example, and then Tech News, and a list of podcasts appears below. (There are so many technology podcasts, and this area is so disorganized, that it helps to know what you're looking for.)

TV Shows. TV Shows is broken down by Genre, TV Shows— "24," "The Daily Show with Jon Stewart," "Desperate Housewives," and "Weeds," for example— and Season. Choose a TV show, and if offered, a list of seasons appears to the right. Choose a season to view individual episodes below (**Figure 5.6**). (If the series doesn't have multiple seasons, just clicking the name of the show will produce the list of available episodes at the bottom of the window.)

Figure 5.6

The Store's no-nonsense browser.

The Results area of these sections is divided into columns titled Name, Time, Artist, Album, Genre, and Price, regardless of whether you're looking at music, movies, music videos, or TV shows. You can sort the list by any of these criteria by clicking the appropriate column head. Click Artist, for example, and the list is sorted alphabetically by artist. Click Time, and the list is sorted by shortest to longest playing time.

tip

You'll notice that a right-pointing arrow appears to the right of entries in some of these views. Clicking this arrow allows you to travel to the page devoted to that item—a great way to explore an album or an artist's catalog after searching for a single song, for example.

Power Search

If you want to be a power shopper, you must learn to take advantage of The Store's Power Search function.

When you click the Power Search link on the main page, you're taken to a page where you can get very specific with your search. Along the top of the window, you find the All, Music, Movies, TV Shows, Music Videos, Audiobooks, Podcasts, and iTunes U entries. Click the appropriate entry, and the fields below change to reflect search criteria. Choose the Music entry, and you can enter information in the Artist, Composer, Song, and Album fields, as well as select a genre from the Genre pop-up menu. Click Movies, and you can search for Movie Title, Actor, Director, Producer, Year, and Rating (all ratings, G, PG, PG-13, or R).

How useful is this feature? If you performed a simple search for the song "Blue Moon" in early autumn 2007 by entering its title in the Search field, you'd be presented with 1,225 matches. Even if you searched by song title, you'll get just over 862 results. Invoke Power Search, however, and you can narrow things down quite nicely.

If you're interested in vocal renditions of "Blue Moon," for example, enter **Blue Moon** in the Song field and then choose Vocal from the Genre pop-up menu. Aha—now you get just 44 matches. Had you entered **Billie Holiday** in the Artist field with the Vocal genre selected, you'd have seen only five matches.

Account

Care to view or edit the information Apple has about you and your credit card? Wonder how you've spent your money at The Store? Want to cancel a movie you've preordered or change your iTunes Plus preference? You can do it all here. When you click the Account link, you'll be asked for your iTunes password. (You can also move to your Apple Account Information page by clicking your account name at the top of the iTunes window.)

Buy iTunes Gifts

Just like a real store, the iTunes Store lets you purchase and redeem gift certificates. It also lets you create a monthly iTunes Store allowance for that someone special. Click this link to be taken to a page where you can do this and more (**Figure 5.7**).

The page works this way:

iTunes Gift Cards. Click this link, and you're taken to the online Apple Store, where you can purchase iTunes gift certificates.

Figure 5.7
iTunes Gifts
page.

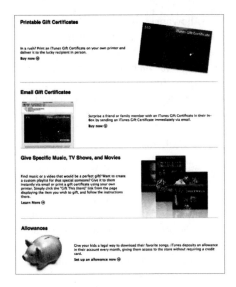

Printable Gift Certificates. This option keeps you in The Store and produces a Printable Gift Certificates pane. Fill in your name and the recipient's name, choose an amount (from $10 to $200), type a personal message, and click Continue to purchase a gift certificate that you can print out and give to your dearest and possibly nearest.

Email Gift Certificates. This option works similarly to printable gift certificates. The difference is that the certificates are sent via email.

Give Specific Music, TV Shows, and Movies. If you've ever listened to an album and thought, "My little snookums would love this!", here's your chance to do something about it. This option lets you give exactly the music, TV show, or movie you'd like.

Allowances. An iTunes allowance can best be described as a gift certificate that keeps on giving. After you create an allowance, the recipient of your largesse will have his or her Store credit bumped up by the amount that you've designated (values include $10 to $100 in $10 increments, $150, and $200) on the first day of each month. Just as when you purchase a gift certificate, your credit card will be charged, not the recipient's.

After you've created an allowance, a new Manage Allowances button appears on your Apple Account Information page. When you click this button, you go to the Edit Allowances page, where you can add allowances or suspend or revoke any that you've created. When you revoke an allowance, any balance placed in the account remains; it won't be credited back to you.

If you think you're going to reinstate that allowance—when your daughter starts making her bed again, for example—use the Suspend button. If you click Remove, you won't be able to put that allowance back into service; you must create a new one. To reactive a suspended account, return to this screen and click the Activate button next to the account name. When you do, a dialog box will appear, asking whether you'd like to send the allowance immediately or wait until the first of the next month.

Redeem

If someone has given you a gift certificate, or you have a prepaid iTunes card, this is where you cash it in. Click the Redeem link, and you'll be taken to the

Redeem Code screen, where you enter the card's code and click Redeem to obtain credits for whatever the card promises.

Support

With this book at your side (or, better yet, open in front of your face), you shouldn't need to click The Store's Support link, but should you come across a problem that's arisen since the publication of this edition, click this link to be taken to Apple's iTunes Store Support page. Here, you'll find answers to frequently asked questions about both iTunes and The Store, as well as customer service, billing, and troubleshooting links.

My Alerts

If you'd like to stay up to date on the releases of favorite artists, you can do so by clicking the Alert Me button on an artist's page. When you do, you can elect to receive email from Apple whenever that artist has released something new. Additionally, when you click the My Alerts link on The Store's home page, you're taken to a page that lists recent releases from artists whose work you've recently purchased.

iTunes also includes a feature for recommending music to you based on the music it knows you own. It's called Just for You. Essentially, iTunes looks at songs you download and recommends music that you're likely to want, based on what you already like. (It also gives you the option of identifying music you own that you didn't get from The Store.) Mostly, it's a hit-or-miss idea. I've received some great recommendations and some that are not so great. You can turn the feature on and off via a Just for You link at the bottom of The Store's main page.

Complete My Album

If you've purchased a couple of tracks from an album and later decide that you'd like to have the entire album, the Complete My Album feature allows you to do so without having to repurchase those tracks. Click this link, and you see a list of albums of which you've purchased portions. Next to each album is the price it will take to complete the album—*Complete My Album for $8.70*, for example.

iTunes Plus

Up until mid-2007, the iTunes Store offered music that was copy-protected with Apple's FairPlay digital rights management (DRM) technology. FairPlay is what limits you to playing your purchased music on five computers. In mid-2007, Apple unveiled iTunes Plus—unprotected music tracks in AAC format encoded at high bit rates (256 Kbps) and sold initially for $1.29 per track, versus 99 cents for protected music tracks. In October 2007, Apple reduced the price of iTunes Plus tracks to 99 cents each.

When you click the iTunes Plus link, the Now in iTunes Plus pane appears (**Figure 5.8**). This pane lists What's Hot, Top Albums, Top Songs, and Featured Albums, all in the iTunes Plus format. At the top of the pane is the Upgrade My Library area with a See Details button. Click the button, and the Upgrade My Library pane tells you how many tracks and music videos currently in your iTunes Library can be upgraded (tracks you've purchased from the iTunes Store). Song upgrades are 30 cents each, album upgrades are 30 percent of the album's current sale price, and music videos cost 60 cents each to upgrade. Regrettably, you can't upgrade individual items; it's all or nothing.

Figure 5.8
iTunes Plus.

When you click the iTunes Plus link, iTunes offers you the opportunity to be offered iTunes Plus tracks by default. If you turn down the offer the first time, you can change your mind by going to your Apple Account Information page (click your account name at the top of the iTunes window, and enter your Apple ID and password), clicking the Manage iTunes Plus button, and enabling the Always Show Me iTunes Plus Music and Music Videos When Available option. Disable this option, and you'll once again be offered the protected version of iTunes' tracks.

tip If iTunes Plus and protected versions of these tracks are both available, why would you ever choose the protected version? Space. Although iTunes Plus offers better encoding, that encoding comes at a price: The files are twice as big. If you want to cram as much music as possible on your computer or iPod, protected tracks may be better choices.

Get the Goods

Now that you have an account and can find your way around The Store, it's time to stop manhandling the merchandise and actually buy something. You'll be amazed by how easy (and addictive) this can be.

The pick-and-pay method

The pick-and-pay method is akin to going to a record store, picking up a CD, taking it to the counter, purchasing the disc, returning to the store to pick another CD, purchasing it, going back to the store once again, and . . . well, you get the idea. You pay as you go. This is how The Store operates by default. Pick-and-pay works this way:

1. Pick your Poison (or Prince, "Prison Break," or *Pirates of the Caribbean*).

Using any of the methods I suggest earlier, locate music, audiobooks, or video that you desperately need to own.

2. Click the Buy button.

To purchase a song or TV episode, click the Buy Song or Buy Episode entry in the Price column that appears in iTunes' main window. To purchase an album, TV season, movie, or audiobook, look near the top of the window for a Buy button. The price of your purchase is listed next to each of these buttons.

 note At times, you can't download an entire album. Instead, The Store may list a partial album—one from which you can purchase only individual songs. Other times, you can't buy certain music tracks individually; you must purchase the entire album.

3. Enter your Apple ID or AOL screen name and password in the resulting window.

4. Click the Buy button.

Just to make sure you weren't kidding around when you clicked the Buy button, a new window asks you to confirm your intention to make your purchase. Should you care to banish this window forevermore, check the Don't Warn Me Again check box.

If you've decided not to purchase the item, click Cancel and go on with your life.

5. Click the Buy button again.

A Downloads entry appears below the Store heading in iTunes' Source list. Click this entry, and you can watch your media download to your computer. If you like, click the Pause button next to anything downloading. You can click the

Resume button that appears in its place to take up the download where you left off. (You might do this to force something you want to listen to *right now* to download before other media.) You're charged for your purchases immediately.

The shopping-cart method

If you intend to bulk up your media library significantly in a single shopping session, you may find the pick-and-pay method tedious. The Store offers an alternative—piling all your music into a single shopping cart and checking out in one fell swoop. To do so, follow these steps:

1. Choose iTunes > Preferences on your Mac or Edit > Preferences on your PC.

2. Click the Store icon in the resulting window.

3. Select the Buy Using a Shopping Cart option.

4. Click OK to dismiss the window.

   A Shopping Cart entry appears in iTunes' Source list.

5. Whirl around The Store until you find something you want to purchase.

   The buttons formerly labeled Buy now read Add.

6. Click the Add button to add an item to your shopping cart.

7. Repeat steps 5 and 6 until you can shop no more.

8. Click the Shopping Cart entry in the Source list.

The main iTunes window displays all the items you've piled into your cart. (Items such as albums and TV seasons that contain multiple tracks or episodes will appear with a triangle next to them. Click the triangle to view the content of the item.)

At the bottom of the window, you'll see the total you'll owe if you proceed. This total does not include sales tax (which—yes—you will be charged).

9. Remove any items you don't want by selecting them and then pressing your computer keyboard's Delete key.

10. Click Buy Now to purchase your media.

Within the shopping cart, you can buy songs or albums individually by clicking Buy Song or Buy Album, or buy everything in the cart by clicking the Buy Now button at the bottom of the iTunes window.

Play with Your Purchase

After the purchased music has found a home on your hard drive, you have several ways to put it to work.

Play it

As you may recall, you are allowed to play purchased media on up to five computers. When you play purchased media for the first time, iTunes checks to see whether the computer is authorized to play it.

If so, the music, movie, audiobook, or TV show plays back with no problem. If the computer hasn't been authorized, you'll be prompted for your Apple ID or AOL screen name and password. That name and password, along with some information that identifies your computer, are sent to Apple, where that Mac or PC is counted against your limit of five authorizations.

If you've used up your authorizations on five other computers, you'll be notified that you must deauthorize one of your computers before you're allowed to play the purchased music. Fortunately, deauthorizing a computer is as simple as choosing Store > Deauthorize Computer in iTunes. When you choose this command, your computer connects to the Internet, and Apple's database is updated to reflect the deauthorization of that particular computer.

After you deauthorize a computer, of course, you can't use it to play back purchased media until you authorize it again. (Yes, this means that if you own more than five computers and intend to play purchased media on all of them, you're going to spend some time playing the deauthorization shuffle.)

Reformatting the computer's hard drive (or replacing that hard drive) does not deauthorize the machine. Before passing your computer along to someone else, be sure to deauthorize it.

Burn it

People play music on all kinds of devices and in all kinds of environments—on computers, boom boxes, home stereos, and portable music players, and in cars, boats, and planes. (I've even seen a system that allows you to play music in your hot tub.) Forcing you to listen to music only on your computer is silly. And because Apple is anything but silly, it made sure that you'd be able to take your purchased music with you on something other than an iPod, MacBook, or Windows PC. It does so by allowing you to burn purchased music to CD.

When you do so, the .m4p files are converted to Red Book audio files—the file format used by commercial audio CDs. These CDs are not copy protected in any way and behave just like regular ol' audio CDs. Pop 'em into a standard CD player and press Play, and out comes the music.

As I indicate earlier in this chapter, burning your music to CD involves a few limitations. You can burn up to seven copies of a particular playlist. If you attempt to burn an eighth copy, you'll be told that you can't. If you alter that playlist after the seventh burn—by adding or removing a song—you can burn another seven copies. Alter that playlist, and you get seven more copies.

To burn media to disc, create a playlist that contains the media you'd like to record to the disc. At the bottom of the playlist, you'll see a Burn Disc button. Insert a blank CD or DVD, and click this button to burn the contents of the playlist onto the disc.

If the playlist contains music only, you'll burn an audio CD. If you're attempting to burn video, that's a different story. iTunes doesn't allow you to burn video—TV shows, music videos, and movies— to discs that can be played on commercial players (such as the DVD player in your living room). Instead, iTunes lets you burn video only as data for purposes of backup.

Book Burning

Unless the narrator of your purchased audio novel or work of nonfiction reads very quickly, the play time for your purchase is likely to be measured in hours. Yet a recordable CD can store only about 80 minutes of audio. How do you cram all that narration onto a single CD?

You can't. When iTunes burns a book to disc, it converts the file to the file format required by audio CDs—a format that consumes 10 MB of hard disk space per minute of stereo audio.

Fortunately, iTunes provides an easy way to record your audio-books to disc. When you select a file that will exceed the record-ing capacity of an audio CD and ask iTunes to burn a disc, the program offers to split the file into lengths that can fit on a CD. (If you must know, each segment is 1 hour, 19 minutes, and 56 seconds.) When iTunes fills one CD, it spits it out and asks for another blank disc. It continues to spit and ask until it finishes burning the entire file to disc.

The resulting discs won't be named in an intuitive way—"War and Peace" I, II, and III, for example. Rather, each will simply read "Audio CD" when you insert it into your Mac or PC. For this reason, you should keep a marker at the ready to label each disc as it emerges from your CD burner.

Limited for Your Protection

With every intention of creating a successful distribution system, Apple has tried to address the desires of both consumers and the music industry. Consumers should be pleased that they're allowed to play music purchased at The Store on a variety of devices: computer; portable music player (the iPod); and any commercial CD player, including the ones in your home stereo, boom box, and car. And the music industry's fears of rampant piracy should be calmed because consumers can play iTunes' protected versions of that music on a limited number of computers; purchased music files are linked to the person who purchased them; only so many copies of a particular playlist can be burned to CD; and by default, the only music player that can play that music is the iPod. (iTunes Plus files are a different matter. They're unprotected, so they can be played on an unlimited number of computers and in any media player that supports the AAC audio file format.)

Following are the specific restrictions Apple imposes on protected purchased music:

- Purchased music is encoded in a protected version of Dolby Laboratories' Advanced Audio Coding (AAC) format, which bears the .m4p extension (versus the .m4a extension of the standard AAC files that iTunes 4 can create). These files are encoded in a way that makes pirating difficult.

- You may play purchased music on up to five computers, which can be a mix of Macs and Windows PCs. All these computers must be authorized by Apple. If you attempt to play purchased music on an unauthorized computer, you'll be instructed to register the computer online before you can play the music. I describe the ins and outs of authorization in "Play it" earlier in this chapter.

continues on next page

Limited for Your Protection   *continued*

- You may burn up to seven CD copies of a particular playlist that contains purchased music. When you change that playlist—add or subtract a song, for example—you may burn another seven copies. Change the playlist again for another seven burns.

- You cannot burn purchased music on CDs formatted as MP3 discs.

- The name and Apple ID of the person who purchased the music are embedded in each purchased piece of media (even iTunes Plus tracks that are otherwise unprotected). Apple does this to discourage buyers from making those songs widely available on the Web (and to trace songs to the rightful owner, should they find their way to the Web).

- Officially, you can download purchased music only one time. In the past, if you lost your music—because your hard drive crashed, for example—you had to purchase it again. You should back up your purchases, of course, but in case you don't, Apple has a secret case-by-case policy whereby you may re-download your purchased media one time per year. Contact iTunes Support at www.apple.com/support/itunes/store/lostmusic/#form if you've been thus afflicted.

- All purchases are final. If you download Highway 9's "Heroine," thinking that it's The Velvet Underground & Nico's "Heroin," you're stuck with it.

- You can play purchased music on as many iPods as you like, as long as those iPods are running iPod Software 1.3 Updater or later. Earlier versions of the iPod software won't recognize AAC-encoded music (either standard AAC encoding or the protected AAC format used for purchased music).

- You can't burn video to a disc that can be played in a commercial player. Burned videos are for backup purposes only.

The iTunes Wi-Fi Music Store

As I say in Chapter 2, the iPod touch has Wi-Fi capabilities for one main purpose: so that you can buy music while on the go. The means for doing so is the iTunes Wi-Fi Music Store, a slimmed-down-in-interface-only version of The Store that's compatible with the iPod touch and with iPhones running software version 1.1.1 or later.

Although the Wi-Fi Music Store's face is far less crowded than that of the grown-up iTunes Store, the music selection is no different. You can choose among the same 6 million-plus tracks in the Wi-Fi Store that you can in the store available via iTunes. The feature works this way.

Browsing the little store

Tap the iTunes icon on the iPod touch's Home screen while you're connected to a Wi-Fi network, and the Wi-Fi Store screen appears. Across the bottom of the screen, you see Featured, Top Tens, Search, and Downloads icons. Here's what to expect.

Featured

When you first enter the Wi-Fi Music Store, you're taken to the Featured area. At the top of the screen are three buttons: New Releases, What's Hot, and Genres. These buttons work much as they do in the same-named areas of the iTunes Store's home page. Tap New Releases, and you see a list of the week's

coolest additions. What's Hot includes popular titles.
Tap Genres, and you'll see a list of available genres.
Tap a particular genre, and you'll see a list of record-
ings for that genre, such as new classical releases.

Top Tens

Tap Top Tens, and you'll find top songs and albums
within particular genres available from the Wi-Fi
Music Store. Tap Rock, for example, and the next
screen includes two large buttons: Top Songs and Top
Albums (**FIGURE 5.9**). Tap one to see the top 10 items
of that kind. When choosing an album, simply tap
its name to view all the tracks on it. If, when viewing
songs, you'd like to see the album a track comes
from, double-tap the track.

Figure 5.9

The iTunes Wi-Fi
Music Store's
Top Tens screen.

Image courtesy of
Apple, Inc.

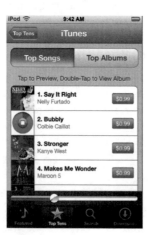

Search

Search is very iPod touch-like. Tap this button, and a Search field appears. Tap this field, and the iPod's keyboard appears. Type a song title, album title, or artist name in this field; as you type, suggestions appear below. When the result you desire appears, tap it.

The resulting screen displays album and song results, showing two albums, a See All Albums link, and 25 songs, followed by a Load 25 More Results link. Tapping See All Albums or Load 25 More Results does exactly what the name suggests.

Downloads

Tap any track, and a 30-second preview streams to your iPod touch and plays. To purchase a track, tap the price. You can also purchase an album by tapping the price next to it.

When you tap a price, it turns into a Buy Now button. Tap that button, and the item swoops down onto the Downloads icon, at which point you're prompted for your iTunes password (the same password you use at the iTunes Store).

 When you type passwords on your iPod touch, they're entered as black dots, so you can't check your work. Type slowly and carefully.

An icon on the Downloads button blinks, indicating the number of items that the iPod is downloading. After the tune has downloaded, you can play it on the iPod. When you next sync your iPod, the tracks you've purchased will be downloaded from the iPod to your computer.

When these tracks are downloaded for the first time, a new playlist appears below the Store heading in iTunes' Source list. That playlist is called Purchased on *nameofipod*, where *nameofipod* is the name of your iPod touch. After these tracks are in your iTunes Library, they behave like any others you own. You can burn them to disc, play them on any of your authorized computers, or play them on any iPods you own.

note If an album you purchase on the iPod touch is bundled with a digital booklet—a file type that the iPod can't download—when you sync the iPod touch with your computer to download that music to it and connect to the iTunes Store, the digital booklet will download to iTunes automatically.

Coming soon: Starbucks

The iPod touch will also display a Starbucks button eventually. As planned by Apple and Starbucks, when your iPod touch is in range of a supported Starbucks outlet, and you have Wi-Fi switched on, a Starbucks icon will appear on the iPod's display. The iPod will be aware of the nearest Starbucks outlet and will tell you the name of the currently playing track, as well as recently played tracks (**Figure 5.10**). Using the Starbucks interface, you'll be able to purchase any of these tracks and, presumably, purchase other music from the Starbucks catalog.

Figure 5.10

Would you like a song to go with that latte?

Image courtesy of Apple, Inc.

As this book goes to press, this service is up and running at Starbucks outlets in Seattle and New York City. Other Starbucks in additional large cities will come online throughout 2007 and 2008. Starbucks expects all outlets to be iPod- and iPhone-compatible in 2009.

6

The Online iPod touch

That blacked-out corner on the back of the iPod touch is more than just decorative. It's the clue that something special lies beneath. And that something special is the touch's wireless networking circuitry—the circuitry your iPod uses to shop at the iTunes Wi-Fi Music Store.

But Wi-Fi is good for more than shopping. In a nearly iPhone-like fashion, your iPod touch can surf the Web and watch streaming YouTube videos. And that's what this chapter is about: the online arm of the iPod touch.

Going on Safari

Your iPod has a real live Web browser, very much like the one on your computer. Follow along as I show you how to use it to best advantage. Let's go surfing!

Importing bookmarks

I know you're eager to start surfing the Web with Safari, but you'll find the experience far more pleasant if you first sync your Safari (Mac) or Safari or Internet Explorer (Windows) bookmarks to your iPod. The process is easy:

1. Jack your iPod into your computer's USB 2.0 port, launch iTunes (if it doesn't launch automatically), select the iPod in iTunes' Source list, and click the Info tab.

2. In the Web Browser area of the window, on a Mac, enable the Sync Safari Bookmarks option (**Figure 6.1**); on a Windows PC, enable the Sync Bookmarks From option and choose either Safari or Internet Explorer from the pop-up menu.

 You must have a copy of Safari for Windows installed for it to appear in this pop-up menu.

Figure 6.1
Syncing Safari within the Mac version of iTunes.

☑ Sync Safari bookmarks

If you use a Web browser other than Safari or Internet Explorer, your browser undoubtedly has an option for exporting its bookmarks. (In Mozilla Firefox, for example, choose Bookmarks > Organize Bookmarks.) In the window that appears, choose File > Export; choose a location for saving your bookmarks; and click Save.

3. Now open Safari and choose File > Import Bookmarks, or fire up Internet Explorer and choose File > Import and Export.

4. Navigate to the bookmarks file you saved.

Your bookmarks are now in a browser that's compatible with the iPod. When you next sync your iPod, those bookmarks will be available to the iPod's copy of Safari.

Surfin' Safari

When you first tap the Safari icon at the bottom of the iPod's Home screen, you may be surprised to see a full (though tiny) representation of a Web page appear before your eyes. Safari on the iPod is nearly the real deal. (In "Safari's limits" later in the chapter, I talk about how that isn't quite the case.)

At first glance, though, it's the real *small* deal. The pages Safari displays on the iPod are Lilliputian at first, but you have ways to make these pages legible:

- **Turn the iPod on its side.** Yes, Safari is one of those iPod touch applications that work in both portrait and landscape orientations. It displays the entire width of a Web page in either view, so when you switch to landscape orientation, you see more detail as the page enlarges to fill the iPod's screen (**FIGURE 6.2**).

Figure 6.2
A Web page in landscape orientation, showing Safari's tool icons.

- **Stretch open the page.** You can enlarge the page by using the stretch gesture. When the page is enlarged, tap and drag to reposition it.

- **Double-tap a column.** Most Web pages include columns of text and graphics. To zoom in on a single column, double-tap it. That column will expand to fill the iPod's screen. To shrink the page to its original size, double-tap the screen again.

- **Double-tap the page.** If a Web page lacks columns, you can still zoom in by double-tapping the page.

Browsing the Web

Like any good browser, Safari provides numerous ways to get around the Web. Let me count the ways.

Getting addressed

Like your computer's Web browser, Safari has an Address field at the top of its main window. To travel to a Web site, tap in this field. When you do, the iPod's keyboard appears. If ever there were an argument for using Safari in landscape orientation, this feature is it, because the iPod's keyboard is far less cramped this way (**FIGURE 6.3**). For just this reason, I wish that other applications supported landscape orientation.

Figure 6.3
The landscape
Safari keyboard.

Type the Web address you want to visit. The iPod and its keyboard make this process as easy for you as possible. To begin with, you needn't type **http:// www**. Safari understands that just about every Web address begins this way and doesn't require you to type the prefix. Just type **examplesite**; then tap the .com key at the bottom of the keyboard (even .com is unnecessary sometimes), and tap Go. In a short time, the page you desire will appear.

Safari offers some other convenient shortcuts for entering addresses. If you've visited the site before, for example, it's likely to be in Safari's History list. If so, just begin typing the address, and it will appear below the Address field (**Figure 6.4**). Tap the address to go to that Web site.

Figure 6.4
The iPod's
History list can
save typing.

 If the Address field is full when you tap it, you can erase its contents quickly by tapping the X icon that appears at the right edge of the field.

 If you're concerned that the contents of your iPod's History list may give others pause, you can clear the list by going to the Safari setting (in the Settings area) and tapping Clear History.

If you need to type a more complex address—
example.com/pictures/vacation.html, for example
—the iPod's default keyboard for Safari can help,
because it includes both period (.) and slash (/) keys.

To leave the keyboard behind without doing
anything, tap the Cancel button. If the page you're
trying to visit is taking too long to load, or if you've
changed your mind about visiting it, just tap the
X that appears next to the Address field while the
page is loading. Safari will stop loading the page. If
you'd like to reload a page that's fully loaded, tap the
Reload icon next to the Address field (the one that
takes the place of the X when a page is completely
loaded).

Search

You can also conduct Google or Yahoo searches from
the keyboard. In portrait orientation, the Search field
appears below the Address field; in landscape orientation, you'll find it to the right of the Address field.
Tap the Search field, enter your query, and then tap
Google or Yahoo (depending on which search engine
you're using).

By default, the iPod uses Google search. To switch to
Yahoo, go to the Settings screen, and tap Safari. Tap
Search Engine and then tap Yahoo.

Links

Links work in Safari just as they do in your computer's browser. Just tap a link to be taken to the associated Web page. Two things are worth noting:

- Safari is sometimes reluctant to use a link while it's still loading a Web page. To speed things up, tap the X icon next to the Address field to stop the current page from loading; then tap the link to load its target immediately.

- When you hover your mouse pointer over a link in your computer's Web browser, you can view information about where that link will take you. The iPod offers a similar, though hidden, capability. Just tap and hold a link, and the name of the link and its URL will appear in a gray bubble (**Figure 6.5**). This feature is useful when you suspect that an innocuous-looking link may take you to a bad place.

Figure 6.5
Preview the location of the link you're about to tap.

Back and forward

Just like your computer's Web browser, Safari has Back and Forward arrows for moving through sites you've visited.

Saved pages

In the bottom-right corner of the Safari screen, you'll see a small Pages icon. Tap it, and you'll see a small representation of the page you're currently viewing. Tap the New Page button in the bottom-left corner of the screen, and you can create a new empty Web page, saving the page you were just viewing in the process (**Figure 6.6**). This feature is the iPod's equivalent of browser tabs.

Figure 6.6
Safari lets you save up to eight pages.

You can repeat this process to save as many as eight pages, and the Pages icon will display the number of pages you've stored. To visit one of your saved pages, tap the Pages icon, and swipe your finger across the display to move back or forward through the saved pages. To view a page full-screen, tap its thumbnail or tap the Done button while its thumbnail is on display. To delete a page, tap the red X in the top-left corner of the page.

 The contents of saved pages aren't cached to the iPod—just their locations. So you won't be able to read them if your iPod isn't connected to a Wi-Fi network or if Wi-Fi is switched off.

Navigating with bookmarks

You heeded my advice to import your computer browser's bookmarks, right? Great. Bookmarks are another fine way to get where you want to go.

Just tap the Bookmarks icon at the bottom of Safari's screen. The Bookmarks screen will appear, replete with your bookmarks organized as they were on your computer. By this, I mean that if you've organized your computer's bookmarks in folders, that's just how they'll appear on your iPod. Bookmarks that you've placed in Safari's Bookmarks Bar are contained in their own folder, named (aptly enough) Bookmarks Bar.

Tap a folder to view the bookmarks it contains. To travel to a bookmark's target page, tap the bookmark.

More on bookmarks

Bookmarks are important-enough components of Safari that they deserve more than this so-far-brief mention. How (for example) do you create bookmarks, organize and edit the ones you have, and delete those you no longer need? Like this.

Creating bookmarks

You've found a Web site you like while surfing with the iPod. To bookmark the site, follow these steps:

1. Tap the plus (+) icon next to the Address field.

2. In the Add Bookmark screen that appears, check the name of the bookmark in the Title field.

If the name is too long for your liking, edit it with the iPod's standard text-editing techniques, or tap the X icon to erase the title and enter one of your own.

3. Tap the Bookmarks entry, and choose a location for your bookmark.

When you do this, a list that contains your bookmarks-folder hierarchy appears. Tap the folder where you'd like to file your bookmark. From now on, this folder is where you'll find that bookmark (**Figure 6.7**).

Figure 6.7
Creating a
bookmark.

4. Tap Save to save the bookmark in this location, or tap Cancel to cancel the bookmarking operation.

Organizing and editing bookmarks

If you're as organized as I am (meaning not very), your bookmarks may be a bit of a mess. Although you're better off organizing the bookmarks on your computer and then syncing them to your iPod, you can organize them on the iPod as well. To do so, follow along:

1. Tap the Bookmarks icon.

2. In the resulting Bookmarks screen, tap the Edit button.

3. To delete an item, tap the red minus (–) icon that appears next to it.

The red minus icon appears next to all entries in the screen save History, Bookmarks Bar, and Bookmarks Menu—in short, all the items you've created but none of the items the iPod requires.

You'll also notice the three-line reposition icon to the right of these marked items, indicating that you can change their positions in the list by dragging the icons up or down. You can also rename your bookmark, change its URL, or file it in a different folder by tapping its name while in editing mode and then making those changes in the resulting Edit Bookmark screen.

Browser as application host

Thanks to the popularity of the iPhone, Web-based applications designed for the iPhone are now beginning to appear, and the iPod touch can take advantage of these applications as well. Just launch Safari and travel to a site that acts as a host for iPhone Web applications, and your iPod gets a whole lot more capable. (Provided, of course, that you're connected to the Web. Break that connection, and these Web-based applications no longer work.)

Some of these Web applications are more useful than others. Some allow you to use instant messaging, access more-advanced calculators and converters, play games, browse online dictionaries, or track flights. Pretty much anything that a person can do in a Web browser is finding its way to the iPhone and now to the iPod touch.

Because books go out of date, rather than recommend specific Web applications that may be bested the day after this book sees print, I'll refer you to the iPhone Application List (**FIGURE 6.8**; http://iphoneapplicationlist.com), which keeps a constantly updated list of iPhone/iPod touch applications. Apple also maintains a list of Web applications at www.apple.com/webapps.

Figure 6.8
iPhone Application List keeps a current list of iPhone and iPod touch Web applications.

Safari and RSS

Safari supports RSS (Really Simple Syndication), the standard for distributing Web headlines. To view collections of these headlines (called *feeds*) on your iPod, all you need to do is locate a page's RSS link and tap it. The page that appears bears a blue bar at the top, along with the name of the site connected to the feed—*Macworld*'s Mac 911 site, for example (**FIGURE 6.9**). The site's headlines appear below the blue bar. Just tap a headline to read the full story.

Figure 6.9
A Safari RSS
feed.

 tip RSS URLs are clumsy to enter yourself; they're long and rarely contain real words. For this reason, bookmarking those that you intend to revisit is a good idea.

Safari's limits

Earlier in this chapter, I hint that although the iPod's version of Safari is about as full featured as you're likely to find on a mobile device, it doesn't have all the capabilities of your computer's browser. The following sections discuss its limitations.

No Flash or Java support

Many modern Web sites greet you with luxurious animations, flickering icons, and animated menus created with Adobe's Web animation design tool, Flash. The iPod doesn't support Flash, and because it doesn't, you may see nothing at all on such a site's home page. Ideally, the designer took into account the fact that not everyone likes (or, in the case of the iPod, can use) Flash and inserted a Skip Animation link that takes you to a Flashless version of the site.

Similarly, many of the movies you find on the Web are Flash-based. If, while traipsing through a Web site, you see a small blue box with a question mark inside it, you're looking at the placeholder for a Flash movie. Tapping that icon will do you no good whatsoever.

The good news is that the iPod will play a lot of QuickTime content (though not all). As the iPod touch and iPhone increase in popularity, Web sites likely will increase their use of QuickTime.

No autofill

You're probably accustomed to your computer's browser automatically filling in information such as your user name, address, and phone number when you visit certain sites. The iPod won't do this—and for good reason. If you lose your iPod, do you really want the person who finds it to log into your Amazon and eBay accounts? I thought not.

No opening links in new pages

I mention earlier in the chapter that although
you can open new Safari pages, you have no
command for tapping a link and opening that link
in a new page, much as you would in a browser
that supports tabs.

No copy, paste, or downloading features

A global issue with the iPod is that you can't copy or
paste anything. And the iPod version of Safari doesn't
support downloading (because in most cases, what
good would it do you?).

No Find

Web pages can be packed with information, and
the iPod's screen is a pretty small place to view that
much content. I'd love to be able to pull up a Search
field and key in a word or phrase that I seek. I can't.

YouTube

I hate to repeat this *just like the iPhone* meme whenever I refer to the iPod touch, but I'm afraid I must
do so again when I say that *just like the iPhone*, the
iPod touch can stream YouTube videos when you're
connected to a Wi-Fi network. Here's how it works.

Tap the YouTube icon on the iPod touch's Home
screen, and you'll see a screen that resembles the
one you view when you enter the iPod's Video area.
This one also has five icons along the bottom.

By default, these icons are Featured, Most Viewed, Bookmarks, Search, and the ever-popular More (**Figure 6.10**).

Figure 6.10
Icons in the
YouTube screen.

You'll find the following when you tap each icon.

Featured

Tap Featured, and you get a list of the 25 YouTube videos that the service believes most worthy of your attention (**Figure 6.11**). To play one, just tap it. The video will stream to your iPod via the Wi-Fi connection. When you scroll to the bottom of the list, you'll see a Load 25 More entry. Tap it, and another 25 videos are added to the list.

Figure 6.11
Featured
YouTube videos.

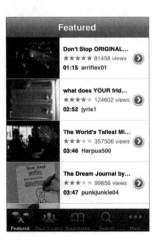

If a video's title, such as *Nora the Piano Cat,* doesn't provide you enough information, feel free to tap the blue icon to the right of the video's title. When you do, you'll see an information screen that tells you the date when the video was added; its category (Drama or Documentary, for example); and its tags, which include anything the poster thought appropriate, such as *poodle, waterslide,* and *ointment* (**Figure 6.12**).

Figure 6.12
A YouTube video information screen.

If you'd like to bookmark the video, tap Bookmark. The video is added to your list of YouTube bookmarks, allowing you to retrieve it easily another time.

The description screen also includes a Related Videos area. If YouTube has videos that it believes are similar in theme to the one you've chosen, it will list them here.

Most Viewed

The Most Viewed icon provides you the opportunity to view YouTube's most popular videos—all videos, or the most viewed today or this week. Like the Featured screen, this one carries a Load 25 More entry at the bottom of the list. To determine whether you watch all, today, or this week's most viewed videos, tap the appropriate icon at the top of the screen.

Bookmarks

As the name hints, here is where your YouTube bookmarks are stored. (The videos themselves aren't stored on the iPod—just the links to them.) To begin streaming one of these videos, just tap its name. To remove a bookmark, tap the Edit icon at the top of the screen, tap the red minus sign (–) that appears next to the entry, and then tap Delete (**Figure 6.13**).

Figure 6.13
YouTube
bookmarks.

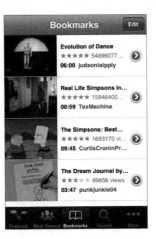

When you're finished removing bookmarks, tap Done, and you'll return to the Bookmarks screen.

These bookmarks apply only to those videos you've bookmarked on your iPod. Yes, you may have bookmarked YouTube videos on your Mac or PC, but no, you can't transfer these bookmarks to your iPod.

Search

You can search YouTube's catalog of videos, and of course, this is the way to go about it. Tap Search, and you get a Search field in return. Tap this field, and up pops the iPod's keyboard. Type a search term—**skateboard** or **Mentos**, for example—and YouTube searches for videos that match your query. Then the service presents a list of 25 videos that it feels match what you're after. If more than 25 videos are available that match your query, your friend the Load 25 More entry appears at the bottom of the list.

More

You've read Chapter 2, right? Then this More icon should be no mystery to you. Tap it, and you're presented three additional choices: Most Recent, Top Rated, and History. Most Recent offers a glimpse of the 25 videos most recently added by YouTube. Top Rated displays YouTube's 25 highest-rated videos. And History details all the videos you've chosen. Yes, *chosen*. You don't have to watch these videos in order for them to appear in your History list. Just choose them, and even if you cancel them before they appear, they'll be part of your iPod's YouTube History. If this list is getting too long, or if you're simply embarrassed by some of the things you've chosen, tap the red Clear icon at the top of the screen. All History entries will disappear.

note The Clear icon is an all-or-nothing affair. Currently, the iPod doesn't provide an option to delete individual videos from the History list.

Playing YouTube videos

To play a YouTube video, tap it, and the video will begin loading in landscape orientation. You'll see the now-familiar video play controls—Back, Play, and Forward—along with a volume slider, timeline, and fill-screen icon. Like the play controls in the iPod's Video area, these controls fade a few seconds after they first appear. To force them to reappear, just tap the iPod's display.

In addition to the play controls, you'll see a Bookmarks icon to the left of the play controls (**Figure 6.14**). Tap Bookmarks, and the currently playing video is added to your YouTube bookmarks.

Figure 6.14
The YouTube play screen.

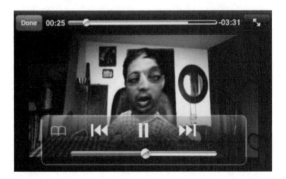

The video will begin playing when the iPod determines that it has downloaded enough data so that the video will play from beginning to end without pausing to download more. When the video concludes, you'll see a description screen for it.

7

The Informational iPod

By now, you probably realize that the iPod is the world's greatest portable music player (and a pretty fair video player too!). But take a quick scroll through the Extras screen of a traditional display-bearing iPod or the Home screen of your iPod touch, and you'll get the idea that the iPod is more than a music player. On those traditional iPods, you'll find the Contacts, Calendars, and Notes entries, which hint that your iPod is ready to offer up a phone number, remind you of an upcoming appointment, or recall your Aunt Vilma's recipe for Swedish meatballs. The iPod touch, while lacking a Notes application, has solid Calendar and Contacts applications.

Though no substitute for a Palm device, the iPod can perform a reasonably convincing impression of a personal information manager. In these pages, I show you how to take best advantage of these features by composing, moving, and synchronizing your contacts, calendars, and notes with your iPod.

Make iContact

There will undoubtedly come a time when a long-forgotten song that shuffles its way around your iPod reminds you of a friend, family member, or deadbeat client. And when that time comes, it may occur to you to get in touch. An iPod packed with contacts can help in these moments. Here's how to make sure those contacts and your iPod see eye to eye.

Syncing contacts to your iPod

All iPods save the iPod shuffle can display contacts. The traditional iPods don't allow you to create contacts on the device itself; instead, you must copy them to the iPod from your computer. The iPod touch can also sync contacts via iTunes, but it lets you create and edit contacts directly on the iPod. To place contacts on your iPod, follow the steps for your operating system in the following sections.

Macintosh

Once upon a time, a program called iSync was responsible for syncing contacts and calendars with an iPod. No longer. iTunes now offers this feature. Here's how it works:

1. Plug your iPod into your Mac.

2. Select your iPod in iTunes' Source list; then click the Contacts tab if you have a traditional iPod or the Info tab if you have an iPod touch.

3. Enable the Sync Address Book Contacts option.

   To place all the contacts in Address Book on your iPod, make sure that the All Contacts option is enabled. If you'd rather place only certain contacts on the iPod, enable the Selected Groups option, and in the list below, choose the groups whose contacts you'd like to copy to the iPod (**Figure 7.1**). You may want only your business contacts or friends and family contacts on your iPod, for example. Grouping those contacts in Address Book and then selecting those groups in iTunes is the way to do it.

Figure 7.1
Selecting groups of contacts in iTunes.

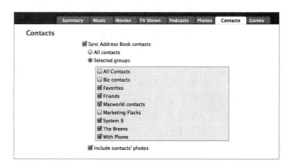

If you plug a 5G iPod, 3G iPod nano, or iPod classic into your Mac, you'll see an option to copy your contacts' photos to the iPod. The iPod touch will always copy a contact's photo if one exists.

4. Click the Apply button at the bottom of the pane.

iTunes will synchronize the selected contacts between your Mac and the iPod.

note In Chapter 4, I mention that the Contacts area offers other options to iPod touch users. To recap, the Contacts area of the Info pane includes the option to put contacts you've created on the iPod touch into an address-book group you specify. Additionally, you have the option to sync your Yahoo Address Book contacts with your iPod touch. On a Macintosh, you find these individual options at the bottom of the Contacts area. In the Windows version of iTunes, you find the Yahoo Address Book option in the Sync Contacts From pop-up menu.

Windows

With iTunes 5, Apple finally brought contact and calendar synchronization to the Windows version of the program. iTunes for Windows will synchronize Windows' Address Book and Outlook contacts and calendars with your iPod. To make it do so, you follow a procedure similar to the one I outline for the Macintosh.

Fire up iTunes with your iPod connected; select your iPod in iTunes' Source list; and, for traditional iPods, click the Contacts tab. If you have an iPod touch, click the Info tab. Within this pane, you can elect to synchronize contacts from Windows Address Book, Outlook, or Yahoo Address Book via a pop-up menu. And as with the Macintosh version of iTunes, you can choose to synchronize all contacts or just selected groups. If you choose Outlook, it will launch automatically. Similarly, iPod touch owners can sync the contacts they create on the touch back to their computer's address book.

tip

You have one additional way to put contacts on a traditional iPod. Mount that iPod as a hard drive, open it, and locate the Contacts folder. Drag into this folder contacts saved in the vCard format (a cross-platform standard supported by all modern contact managers, computers, and PIMs). When you unmount your iPod, the contacts will appear just as though you'd synced them via iTunes.

Managing contacts on the iPod touch

I promised in Chapter 2 that I would discuss the ins and outs of contacts on the iPod touch. And why does this topic deserve a section of its own? Unlike any other iPod, the iPod touch allows you to create and edit contacts, and that capability takes some explaining. Here's the lowdown.

Handling the people you know

Tap the Contacts icon, and you see a list of your contacts in alphabetical order (**FIGURE 7.2**).

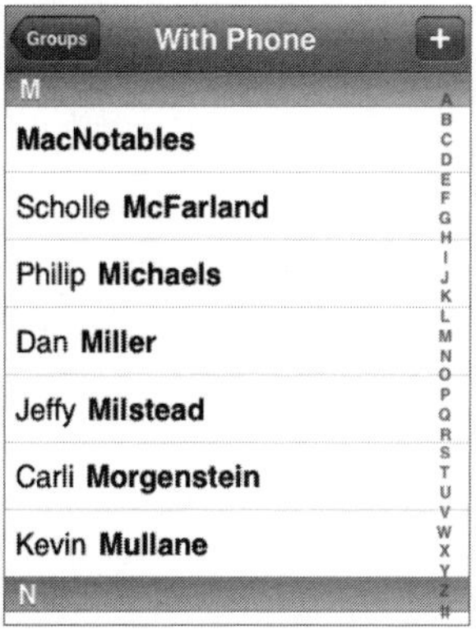

Figure 7.2
The Contacts screen.

Groups	With Phone	+

M

MacNotables

Scholle **McFarland**

Philip **Michaels**

Dan **Miller**

Jeffy **Milstead**

Carli **Morgenstein**

Kevin **Mullane**

N

This list works very much like any long list of items you see in the iPod's Music area. A tiny alphabet runs down the right side of the screen. Tap a letter to move immediately to contacts whose names (first or last, depending on how you've configured name sorting in Contacts preferences) begin with this letter.

When you tap a name, you're taken to that contact's Info screen (**Figure 7.3**).

Figure 7.3
A contact's Info screen.

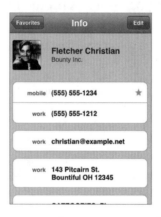

Here, you can find information including the following:

- Photo—a photo you've added in Address Book on a Mac or by tapping Add Photo and choosing a picture from your Photos collection

- Name

- Title

- Company

- Phone number—including Mobile, Home, Work, Main, Home Fax, Work Fax, Pager, Home Phone 2, Work Phone 2, and Other headings, as well as a Custom Label option so you can enter labels such as *Dirigible* or *Private Train Car*

- Email address—including Home, Work, and Other options

- URL (for the contact's Web site)

- Home address

- Work address

- Other address

- Birthday

- Notes

- Other fields—including Prefix, Middle Name, Suffix, Nickname, Department, and Anniversary Date

You won't necessarily find all these entries in a contact's Info screen; this list just shows you what's possible to include.

Organizing contacts in groups

Although you see a list of all your contacts when you first tap Contacts, the Contacts application has an organizational layer above the main list. If, in the Info iPod preference within iTunes, you've chosen to sync your address book with select groups of contacts, or if your full address book contains groups of contacts, those groups will appear in the Groups screen, which you access by tapping the Groups button in the top-left corner of the Contacts screen (**Figure 7.4**).

Figure 7.4
The Groups screen.

Organizing in groups makes a lot of sense if you have loads of contacts. Although Apple made traversing a long list of contacts as easy as possible, easier still is tapping something like a Family group and picking Uncle Bud's name out of a list of 17 beloved relatives.

Making contacts

The best way to become familiar with the iPod's contacts is to make some of your own. To do that now, tap Contacts on the Home screen and then the plus (+) icon in the top-right corner of the iPod's screen.

The New Contact screen contains the entries I listed earlier (**FIGURE 7.5**). To add information to one of these fields, tap the field or the green plus icon to its left. In the resulting screen, you'll find a place to enter the information.

Figure 7.5
The New
Contact screen.

Here are the special features of each screen:

Add Photo. Tap this entry, and you're taken to your Photos library, where you can select a picture. Just as you can when creating a wallpaper image, you can move and scale these images and then tap Set Photo to attach them to the contact.

Name. In this screen, you enter first, last, and company names. Tap Save to return to the New Contact screen.

Add New Phone. As the name says, this field is where you add a phone number. In the Edit Phone screen, you tap in the number from the keypad and then choose the kind of phone number: Mobile, Home, Work, Main, Fax, Pager, or Other.

note The numeric keypad contains a key that reads +*#. Tap it, and those three characters appear on the keypad's bottom three keys. What good are they? They're used by automated answering systems for performing certain functions. Some phone systems, for example, require that you press the pound key and then a key combination to unblock a hidden phone number or append an extension. Another character can introduce a pause between numbers.

Add New Email. Enter your contact's email address here. The iPod's keyboard in this screen contains at (@), period (.), and .com keys to make the process easier.

Add New URL. Same idea here. The more-convenient keyboard is in evidence, but instead of an @ symbol, you'll find period (.), slash (/), and .com. You can apply a Home Page, Home, Work, or Other label to the URL.

note URLs contained within contacts are live, meaning that if you're connected to a Wi-Fi network and tap a URL, Safari will open and take you to that Web page.

Add New Address. In the United States, the default Edit Address screen contains two Street fields and areas for City, State, and Zip. Ah, but tap the country field and choose a different nation from the list that appears, and these fields change. If you choose Ukraine, for example, the bottom fields change to Postal District, Province, and Postal Code. Tap the Location icon next to the Country icon to choose the nature of this address: Home, Work, or Other.

Add Field. Tap Add Field, and you can add more fields to a contact's Info screen. These fields include Prefix, Middle Name, Suffix, Phonetic First and Last Name, Nickname, Job Title, Department, Birthday, Date (Anniversary and Other are the options), and Note. Both the Birthday and Date screens contain the iPod's spinning date wheel for selecting the month, day, and year quickly.

Working with existing contacts

When you have contacts on your iPod, you can delete them, edit the information they contain, or use that information to perform other tasks on your iPod.

To delete a contact, just tap the Edit icon that appears in the contact's Info screen, scroll to the bottom of the screen, and tap the big red Delete Contact button. You'll be asked to confirm your choice.

To edit a contact, tap that same Edit icon in the contact's Info screen, and make the edits you want (**Figure 7.6**). You can add information by tapping a field that begins with the word *Add* (or just tap its green plus icon). To delete information, tap the red minus icon next to the information and then tap the now-revealed Delete button. When you finish editing the contact, tap Done.

Figure 7.6
An elongated view of the contact edit screen.

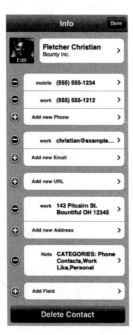

Make a Date

Apple would have looked mighty foolish adding calendaring capabilities to the iPod without also providing Mac users a calendar application. It did so by releasing iCal, a free, basic calendar application that runs under Mac OS X 10.2 and later.

iCal isn't the only Macintosh application that's compatible with the iPod, however. Both Microsoft Entourage (part of Microsoft Office X and Microsoft Office 2004 for Macintosh) and Palm's Palm Desktop 4.x can also export iPod-compatible calendar files (files saved in the vCal format).

Windows users can create iPod-friendly calendar files, too; unfortunately, they can't do it with an Apple application. Windows users who have a copy of Microsoft Office will discover that Outlook can export calendar files that are compatible with the iPod, as can Palm's Palm Desktop 4.x.

Syncing events with traditional iPods

The following sections show you how to make the most of calendars with your computer's common calendar applications and a traditional, display-bearing iPod.

iCal (Mac OS X 10.2 or later)

Although you can move iCal calendars into your traditional iPod by selecting a calendar in iCal, choosing File > Export, and dragging the resulting calendar file into the iPod's Calendars folder, why bother when iTunes provides a more expedient method? To use iTunes, just follow these steps:

1. Plug your iPod into your Mac.

2. Select your iPod, and click the Contacts tab.

3. Enable the Sync iCal Calendars option.

   This is sounding familiar, right? Yes, it's very much like moving contacts via iTunes. Similarly, you can choose to synchronize All Calendars or Selected Calendars. When you choose the latter option, just check the boxes next to the calendars you want to copy to the iPod, and click OK.

4. Click the Apply button.

   iTunes will synchronize the selected calendars between your Mac and the iPod.

Outlook (Windows)

You guessed it—syncing calendars on a Windows PC is darned similar to doing it on the Mac. The major difference is that there is no iCal for Windows. Instead, you have the option to synchronize all your Outlook calendars or just selected calendars.

Calendar and the iPod touch

The iPod touch is different from the traditional iPods in just about every way, and its calendar capabilities are no exception. Follow along to touch your events.

Viewing events

Calendar is capable of displaying events in three views: List, Day, and Month. They're laid out like so.

Month. Tap Calendar, and by default, you'll see this month's calendar, with today's date highlighted in blue. Other days maintain a gray, businesslike appearance. Tap another day, and it adopts the blue box, while the present day gains a deeper gray hue. To return to the current day, tap it (if you're viewing the current month), or tap the Today button in the top-left corner of the screen. To move to the next or previous month, tap the Next or Previous arrow, respectively, next to the month heading. To scan ahead faster, tap and hold one of these arrows.

Any days on the calendar that have events appended to them bear a small black dot below the date. Tap a day with a dot, and the events for that day appear in a list below the calendar, each preceded by its start time (**FIGURE 7.7**). Tap an event in this list, and you're taken to the Event screen, which details the name and location of the event, its date, its start and end times, and any notes you've added to the event.

Figure 7.7
Month view
with an event.

Today	List	Day	Month
◄	**January 2008**		►
Sun	Mon	Tue	Wed	Thu	Fri	Sat
30	31	1	2	3	4	5
6	7	8	9	10	11	12
13	**14**	15	16	17	18	19
20	21	22	23	24	25	26
27	28	29	30	31	1	2

All-day   **Macworld Expo**

Day. Tap the Day view button, and as you'd expect, you see the day laid out in a list, separated by hours. The day of the week and its date appear near the top of the screen. To move to the previous or next day, tap the Previous or Next arrow, respectively. To scan back or forward more quickly, tap and hold the appropriate arrow.

Events appear as blue-gray bars in the times they occupy, and are labeled with the name of the appointment and its location (**Figure 7.8**). Just as with events in Month view, tap them to reveal their details.

Figure 7.8
Day view with
two events.

List. List view shows a list of all the events on your calendar, separated by gray bars. Each gray bar bears the day's abbreviated name (Fri or Mon, for example) and the month, date, and year of the event. The event's title appears just below, preceded by its start time. Once again, tap an event to view its details (**FIGURE 7.9**).

Figure 7.9
List view.

Living with limits

Unfortunately, the iPod touch holds just a single calendar. Although you can ask iTunes to sync multiple calendars to the iPod (if you're using a Mac, your iCal Work and Home calendars, for example), all events go into that one calendar. For this reason, I've created a special iCal iPod touch calendar where I place events that I want to carry with me.

Notes-worthy Feature

If you select Notes in the Extras screen on a traditional Dock-connector iPod (notes aren't supported
on earlier iPods, the iPod touch, or the screenless iPod
shuffle) and then select the Instructions entry, you'll
learn that you can view plain-text notes on your iPod.
But there's more to know about Notes than that:

- **Notes are strictly limited to 4 Kbits.** If a note
  exceeds 4 Kbits (4,096 bytes), the excess text is
  cut off.

- **The iPod can hold up to 1,000 notes.** If the iPod's
  Notes folder contains more than 1,000 notes, only
  the first 1,000 notes are displayed. (The first 1,000
  are determined by alphabetical order rather than
  creation date.)

- **Notes are cached in memory.** After you've viewed
  a note, its contents are stored in a 64 KB memory
  cache. This cache is useful because it allows the
  iPod to display the note without spinning up the
  hard drive on those iPods that have a hard drive,
  thereby extending the battery charge. When the
  cache overflows (because you've read more than
  64 KB of data into it), the oldest notes are given
  the boot to make room for the information being
  copied into the cache.

- **Notes support a very basic set of HTML tags** (the
  Hypertext Markup Language codes used to create
  Web pages). These tags allow you to create notes
  that link to other notes or to songs on your iPod.

You may be thinking, "Well, ain't this ducky, Chris, but other than providing a place to store directions to Auntie Di's suburban manse or the French translation of 'I'm sorry, but this éclair appears to be stuffed with haddock,' what earthly use are these notes?"

Notes can be linked via the HTML tags I mention earlier, thereby opening a host of possibilities. Museums, for example, can use notes that are linked to one another (and to the iPod's photos, album art, and audio and video tracks) to create audio guides, with notes that link to audio descriptions of paintings in a particular gallery. And real estate agents can offer potential buyers iPod-led tours of new properties.

I fear that I don't have the space necessary to provide instructions for creating these rich notes. Fortunately, Apple offers a guide for doing this at http://developer.apple.com/ipod/iPodNotesFeatureGuideCB.pdf.

8

Tips and Tricks

You're far enough along in this little guide to understand that the iPod and iTunes hold more secrets than just Rip, Click, and Play. This dynamic duo have other wonders to behold if you know how to unleash them. And that's exactly the point of this chapter: to shed light on the lesser-known marvels of the iPod and iTunes.

Let the magic begin.

Move Media off the iPod

To deter piracy, iTunes and the iPod were designed so that media would travel in one direction only: from the computer to the iPod. When you double-click a traditional iPod mounted on a computer, you'll find no folder within that holds the device's music or movies. Yet this material has to be there somewhere.

It is. It's invisible.

When Apple designed the original iPod's copy-protection scheme, it did so understanding one of the fundamental laws of this new millennium: That which can be locked will be unlocked (by a 12-year-old boy).

Rather than dump millions of dollars into a compli-cated copy-protection scheme—which would almost immediately be broken by one of those wily 12-year-olds—the company did the wise thing and protected the iPod in such a way that honest folks aren't tempted to pilfer music and movies off another person's iPod. The company's engineers did nothing more than make the iPod's Music folder invisible (and yes, movies are stored in the Music folder too). Therefore, the trick to getting the media off the iPod is accessing this invisible folder.

note **Regrettably, Apple has locked down the iPod touch in a serious way. As this book goes to press, there's only one way to copy music from an iPod touch to your computer (Mac only); I cover it in the "More-refined methods" section.**

Brute-force techniques

Though fairly graceless, one of the easiest ways to retrieve your media from a traditional iPod is to make the iPod's Music folder visible and drag it over to your computer's desktop. Then simply add that folder (and the music within) to iTunes by dragging the folder into iTunes' main window or by choosing File > Add to Library in iTunes. Here's how to do this on either a Mac or a Windows PC.

Macintosh

The Mac doesn't include a utility for making invisible files visible, so you must download one. My favorite tool for this job is Marcel Bresink's free TinkerTool (www.bresink.de/osx/TinkerTool.html). After you've downloaded TinkerTool, follow these steps:

1. Plug in the iPod.

   If iTunes doesn't launch automatically, launch it. If the music library on your iPod is not linked to iTunes' music library (as would be the case when you're restoring your music library from your iPod to a fresh copy of iTunes installed on a refor- matted drive), iTunes will ask if you'd like to sync the contents of the iPod with the contents of the iTunes Library. Click Cancel.

2. Select the iPod in iTunes' Source list, and make sure that the Summary tab in iTunes 7's main window is selected.

3. Enable the Manually Manage Music option, as well as the Enable Disk Use option.

4. Launch TinkerTool, and click the Finder tab.

5. Enable the Show Hidden and System Files option.

6. Click Relaunch Finder.

7. Move to the Finder, and double-click the iPod's icon on the Desktop.

You'll discover that several more items now appear in the iPod window. Among them is a folder called iPod_Control.

8. Double-click the iPod_Control folder.

Inside the iPod_Control folder, you'll find a variety of folders. The one you care about is Music.

9. Drag the Music folder to your Mac's Desktop to copy it to your computer.

As the name implies, this folder is where music is stored on the iPod.

In earlier versions of iTunes, you could simply drag this Music folder to iTunes' main window, and the music within it would be copied to iTunes' music library. This is no longer the case. You must now open the Music folder, open the folders within (the names of all these folders begin with the letter *F*), and then drag the contents of the folders into the Library entry in iTunes' Source list.

The songs you copied from the iPod will be added to iTunes. If you're a tidy type, before copying those files to iTunes, open iTunes' preferences, click the Advanced tab, and make sure that the Keep iTunes Music Folder Organized and Copy Files to iTunes

Music Folder When Adding to Library options are enabled. Enabling these options will organize your iTunes Library in the way iTunes prefers.

Windows

At the risk of making my Windows readers feel like second-class citizens, please follow the first three steps outlined in the instructions for Mac users. Once you've done that:

1. Double-click the My Computer icon on the desktop.

2. Locate your iPod in the window that appears, and select it.

3. In the My Computer window, choose Tools > Folder Options.

4. Click the View tab in the Folder Options window that appears.

5. Below the Hidden Files and Folders entry, enable the Show Hidden Files and Folders option; then click Apply to reveal the hidden files.

6. Dismiss the Folder Options windows by clicking the OK button.

7. Double-click the iPod's icon in the My Computer window.

8. Sorry about the return to second-class-citizen status, but please follow steps 8 and 9 of the Macintosh instructions in the preceding section.

9. When the Music folder is on the desktop, right-click the folder, select Properties from the contextual menu, uncheck the Hidden option in the Attributes area of the General tab, and click Apply.

10. In the Confirm Attributes Change window that appears, make sure that the Apply Changes to This Folder, Subfolders, and Files option is checked; then click OK.

The folder and all the items in it are now visible and can be dragged into the iTunes Library.

Although the music files bear a seemingly incomprehensible four-letter title (AHLK.m4a, for example) when viewed outside iTunes, their titles will appear properly after you've brought them into iTunes.

More-refined methods

Scan sites such as hotfiles.com and VersionTracker (http://www.versiontracker.com), and you'll discover a host of utilities designed to pull media off your iPod and onto your computer. Some of these utilities are more sophisticated than others, allowing you to copy not only the music the iPod carries, but its playlists as well. Here are a few of my favorites.

Macintosh

Whitney Young's free Senuti (www.fadingred.org/ senuti) offers a straightforward interface for moving media off your iPod (**FIGURE 8.1**). Like similar utilities, it allows you to select tracks and videos on the iPod and then copy them to a location of your choosing. Unlike some other utilities, Senuti lets you copy not only videos, single songs, and songs grouped by artist and album, but also complete playlists from the iPod.

Figure 8.1

Senuti is a great (and free) tool for moving music from your traditional iPod to a Mac.

tip

Apple has locked down the iPod touch more than it has other iPods, so getting media off it is a bit trickier. As this book goes to press, one tool can do it, but only on a Macintosh. That tool is Ecamm Networks' $10 iPhoneDrive (www.ecamm.com/mac/iphonedrive). It will mount your iPod as a hard drive, at which point you can look into the media area; select music, videos, and photos; and copy them to your computer's hard drive. I suspect that other tools will be available by the time you read this book.

Windows

WindSolutions' $20 CopyTrans (www.copytrans.net) does much of what Senuti does, but without Senuti's attractive price. It too features an iPod-like interface and can copy music as well as video from the iPod to a Windows PC.

iPodSoft's $15 iGadget (www.ipodsoft.com) can also move media from the iPod to your PC, exporting movies, single songs, or playlists. In addition, it can transfer data such as weather forecasts, local movie times, driving directions, and RSS news feeds. This information appears in the iPod's Notes area.

Get the Greatest Charge out of Your iPod

No, I'm not being colloquial. I don't intend to tell you how to get the greatest thrill out of your iPod, but how to coax the longest play time from a single battery charge.

Keep it warm (but not too warm). Lithium-ion batteries perform at their best when they're oper-ated at room temperature. If your iPod is cold, warm it up by putting it under your arm (which, with a really chilly iPod, is an invigorating way to wake up in the morning). And keep your iPod out of your car's hot glove compartment.

Flip on the Hold switch. If you accidentally turn your traditional iPod on while it's in a pocket, purse, or backpack, you'll be disappointed hours later when you discover that its battery has been drained by playing only for itself. An engaged Hold switch will keep this from occurring. (The iPod touch automati-cally locks when it goes to sleep.)

Don't touch it. OK, that's a bit extreme. What I really mean is that every time you press—or, in the case of the iPod touch, tap—a button, the iPod has to make an additional effort, which drains the battery more quickly.

Turn off EQ and Sound Check, and don't use back-lighting. These extras—particularly backlighting—eat into your battery's charge.

Load your iPod with songs smaller than 9 MB. The more often your iPod's hard drive spins up and its memory cache fills and empties, the more quickly its battery is drained. Files that exceed 9 MB force more frequent hard-drive spins and cache activity. For this reason, you'll get more play time from your iPod if your song files are in the compressed AAC and MP3 formats versus the big ol' AIFF, WAV, and Apple Lossless formats.

Turn down the brightness control. The 5G iPods updated with the latest iPod software include bright-ness controls, as do the 3G iPod nano, iPod classic, and iPod touch. The brighter your iPod's display, the faster your battery drains.

Convert Video for iPod

The iTunes Store offers a growing trove of TV shows and movies you can purchase for viewing on your video-capable iPod, but chances are good that you have some personal videos you'd like to load onto the device too—either homemade digital video from your camcorder or possibly commercial movies you already own and don't care to repurchase from The Store.

note A nonlawyer's free legal advice (and you know what that's worth): Copying media you don't own is illegal, whether or not you profit from your efforts; and the legality of duplicating copyrighted DVDs, even those you own, is murky territory. (The law allows you to make a single copy of each DVD for archival purposes. Does a copy made to your iPod count? Does a copy cease to be archival if you watch it?) Use your own judgment in following the advice in this section.

Rip commercial DVDs

Video-capable iPods recognize two related forms of digital video, generically called H.264 and MPEG-4. Generally speaking, the newer H.264 option is better for iPods; it includes support for high-definition video, and it generally yields higher-quality video and smaller files than MPEG-4. To convert commercial DVD video to these formats, you face a couple of challenges: removing the copy protection and then creating a video that works with the iPod. Tools available for the Mac and for Windows PCs can do the job.

For Mac users, that tool is HandBrake (http:// handbrake.m0k.org). This open-source DVD-to-MPEG-4 converter not only skirts commercial DVDs' copy protection, but also converts files to a format that's compatible with the iPod. The latest version of HandBrake includes a preset for the iPod. Just choose this preset, and HandBrake will rip a file compatible with your iPod (**Figure 8.2**).

Figure 8.2
HandBrake.

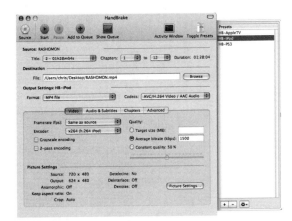

A version of HandBrake is available for Windows, but it doesn't work with copy-protected DVDs. After you use a utility such as DVD Shrink (www.dvdshrink.org) or DVDDecrypter (www.mrbass.org/dvdrip) to remove the copy protection, HandBrake for Windows will convert the resulting video for iPod.

Convert home video

iTunes provides a way to convert your unprotected homemade video for iPod use. Just drag your movie into iTunes, select it, and choose Advanced > Convert Selection for iPod.

Shift Your iTunes Library

It may not happen today, tomorrow, or next year, but if you're an iTunes enthusiast, your computer's startup drive will eventually be so choked with media that you won't have room for anything else. When this happens, you'll want to move your iTunes Library to another hard drive. Here's how:

1. Create a new location for your media files—in a folder on an additional internal or external hard drive, for example.

2. Launch iTunes, and choose iTunes > Preferences (Mac) or Edit > Preferences (Windows) to open the iTunes Preferences window.

3. Click the Advanced pane and then the General tab, and click the Change button.

4. In the resulting Change Music Folder Location dialog box, navigate to the new location you just created, and click Choose.

5. In that same Advanced pane, enable the Keep iTunes Music Folder Organized and Copy Files to iTunes Music Folder When Adding to Library options (**Figure 8.3**); then click OK to dismiss the Preferences window.

Figure 8.3
iTunes'
Advanced
preference
settings.

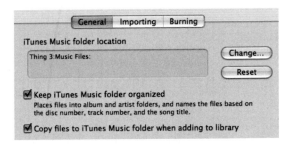

6. Choose Advanced > Consolidate Library.

As the dialog box that appears indicates, this command will copy all your media files to the iTunes Music folder—a version of that Music folder that now exists on another drive.

7. Click Consolidate.

iTunes copies not only your files to the destination you designated, but also your library's playlists. (Ratings will be maintained as well.)

note With iTunes 7, you can span an iTunes Library across volumes. To do this, open the Advanced pane of the iTunes Preferences window, select the General tab, click the Change button, and designate a new iTunes Music folder location. With the Copy Files to iTunes Music Folder When Adding to Library option off, iTunes will look to this new folder while also maintaining contact with the old one; you can still play the files from your old iTunes Music folder as well as the new one. When you add new music, it will be added to the new location.

Spread the Word

If you want to alert your pals to your new favorite podcast, there's no need to send them to the iTunes Store. Just select Podcasts in iTunes' Source list, choose the show title (but not a particular episode) you want to share with your friends, and drag it to your computer's desktop. The title will be turned into a podcast subscription file (with a .pcast extension). Email this file to your nearest and dearest. When they drag the file into iTunes (or double-click it), they'll be subscribed to the podcast that's linked to the file.

iPod shuffle, Autofill, Podcasts, and You

iTunes does its best to cram the most music it can onto an iPod shuffle. For this reason, a shuffle won't play Apple Lossless files, which tend to take up a lot of space; neither will it automatically download AIFF files to the shuffle (though these files will play on the 2G and 3G shuffle). Likewise, the Autofill feature that's available when you plug in an iPod shuffle won't add audiobooks or podcasts (which can also be meaty) to the shuffle, even if you've gathered those podcasts into a playlist.

You can, of course, add those files to the shuffle by dragging them to the shuffle entry in iTunes' Source list. Alternatively, if you convert podcasts to a different format—AAC, for example—Autofill will have no objection to pulling them over to the iPod automatically.

To perform that conversion, go to the Importing tab of the Advanced pane in iTunes' Preferences window; select the encoder you'd like to use; then choose Advanced > Convert Selection to *XXX* (where *XXX* is the encoder you've chosen in the Importing tab). With the right configuration—such as the AAC encoder, using the Spoken Podcast setting from the Setting pop-up menu—you can create files smaller than the originals.

note

When you convert these files, they'll lose any chapter marks they had, and the podcasts will no longer be bookmarkable. To make a podcast bookmarkable, select it, choose File > Get Info, click the Options tab, enable the Remember Playback Position option, and click OK.

Add Radio Stations to iTunes

Select the Radio entry in iTunes' Source list, and if your computer is connected to the Internet, you'll discover that you can listen to streaming Internet radio broadcasts in just about every genre imaginable. From all appearances, only Apple can add stations to these radio listings. But appearances can be deceiving; you can add other stations to the iTunes Library and to playlists of your own.

To do so, find a station you want streamed to your computer. The free SHOUTcast (www.shoutcast.com) provides a load of links to streaming stations. Click the link to the station, and download the resulting .pls (playlist) file to your computer. If the playlist doesn't open in iTunes automatically, drag the file into iTunes' main window; it will appear in the iTunes Library as an MPEG audio stream, which you can listen to (**Figure 8.4**). Now you can create a new playlist and drag your stations into it, thus giving yourself access to all your custom stations from one location.

Figure 8.4
Streaming Internet radio stations in iTunes.

☑ 🛜 FunkyHotMix – Hot Mix Radio 100% Disco F...	Contin...
☑ 🛜 Groove Salad: a nicely chilled plate of ambi...	Contin...
☑ 🛜 KCRW Music	Contin...
☑ 🛜 KCRW Simulcast	Contin...
☑ 🛜 KCSM Jazz 91 * The Bay Area's Jazz Stati... ⊕	Contin...
☑ 🛜 S K Y . F M – Mostly Classical – Listen and R...	Contin...
☑ 🛜 SmoothLounge.com – Music To Move You (...	Contin...
☑ 🛜 1.FM – Otto's Baroque Musick	Contin...
☑ 🛜 1.FM – The Chillout Lounge	Contin...

Make Allowances

If you're like a lot of iTunes Store customers, you occasionally bust your budget and purchase more music than you should. To help you keep your spending in check, let me show you how to give yourself an iTunes allowance.

As I mention in Chapter 5, the iTunes Store allows you to give other users a music allowance—in amounts from $10 to $200—that renews automatically each month. Regrettably, Apple forbids you to create an allowance for the account you've logged in with.

The trick, therefore, is to create a second Apple ID that confers an allowance on your original ID. It works this way:

Launch iTunes, and travel to the iTunes Store via the iTunes Store link. If you're signed into The Store, choose Store > Sign Out. Then choose Store > Sign In (or click the Sign In button in the top-right corner of the iTunes window). In the window that appears, click Create New Account. Walk through the steps necessary to create a new account.

 You can create up to five Apple IDs with a single credit-card number. Your request to create a sixth account tied to a particular credit-card account will be denied.

After you've signed in with the new account, click the Buy iTunes Gifts link on The Store's main page; then click the Set up an Allowance Now link on the resulting page. Navigate through the allowance-creation screens, and enter your original Apple ID as the recipient of the allowance. You'll have the option to start an allowance right now or to have the allowance kick in at the beginning of the next month.

The last step, of course, requires a measure of self-control. When you've used up your monthly allowance, stop buying music!

iPod touch Text Tips

The one iPod touch feature that frustrates the greatest number of people is text entry. These tips will help make you a better iPod typist.

Keep going

Typing on the iPod's keyboard isn't like typing on your computer keyboard—a process in which you type, make a mistake, backspace to correct the mistake, and continue typing. Use that technique on the iPod touch, and you'll go nuts making the constant corrections.

Typing the first letter correctly is important, as mistyping that first letter is likely to send the iPod's predictive powers in the wrong direction. But after that, get as close as you can to the correct letters and continue typing even if you've made a mistake. More often than not, the iPod's predictive typing will correct the mistake for you (**Figure 8.5**).

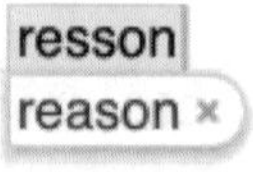

Sure, you may need to go back and correct a word or two in a couple of sentences by pressing and holding the display to bring up the magnifying-glass icon, but doing this for two mistakes is far more efficient than retyping half a dozen words.

Adjust your aim

When you start typing on your iPod touch, you'll discover that your aim is off. Because I'm right-handed, for example, I tend to tap the right edge of a letter and often type the letter to its right instead.

Figure 8.5
More often than not, the iPod knows what you meant to type.

resson
reason ×

The iPod, however, likes its letters tapped right in the middle. Similarly, I aim a little low in lists.

If you find that you're missing more often than you hit, consciously type to the opposite side of the key or command, or try typing with the entire pad of your finger rather than just the tip. Chances are that you'll nail what you're trying to type.

Move to the correct letter

In one specific instance, you'll need to type as carefully as possible: when you're entering a password. As I've mentioned elsewhere, for security reasons the iPod enters dots in a password field rather than characters, so you don't have the luxury of going back to correct your work, because you can't see where you've made a mistake.

For this reason, when you're entering passwords (or just typing carefully), tap a character and wait for the letter to pop up on the display. If you've hit the wrong character, keep your finger on the display and move it to the correct character. Only when you release your finger does the iPod accept the character.

Adjust the dictionary

Irked because the iPod invariably suggests *candle* when you intended to type *dandle*? You have the power to modify the iPod's built-in dictionary. If you type *d-a-n-d-l-e*, but the iPod displays *candle*, simply tap the *candle* suggestion, and it disappears. Then finish typing.

When you next get a good way into typing *dandle*, the iPod will propose it as the word to use. When it does, just tap the spacebar to autocomplete the word. The iPod's not stupid, so it won't suggest *dandle* when you next type *candle*, but it may not autocomplete *candle* that first time. In subsequent entries, however, it probably will.

Avoid unnecessary capitalizations and contractions

The iPod tries to make as much sense as possible from your typing. When it's willing to, let it carry the load. You probably won't type the letter *i* all by itself unless you mean *I*, for example. The iPod knows this and will make a lone *i* a capital *I*. Similarly, type *ill*, and even if you're trying to say that you're not feeling well, the iPod will suggest *I'll*. Conversely, if you're feeling fine, the iPod allows you to type *well* without suggesting *we'll*. Knowing that both *its* and *it's* are common, the iPod will never suggest the contraction.

Rule of thumb: When a word that can also be spelled as a contraction is tossed at the iPod, it will suggest the more commonly used word.

9

Troubleshooting Your iPod

I regret to report that—except for you, dear reader, and me—nothing is perfect. No, not even the iPod. Whereas it may tick happily along one day, the next day, its menu structure is a mess; it refuses to start up when you're sure it has a full battery; or when it does start up, it displays an icon indicating that it is feeling far from well. In this chapter, I look at the common maladies that afflict the iPod and what, if anything, you can do about them.

You've heard it often enough by now: The traditional iPods and iPod touch differ to the point where it makes little sense to discuss them in the same breath. With that in mind, I devote the first part of this chapter to the iPod design of old before embarking on the brave new world of the iPod touch.

Problems and Solutions: Traditional iPods

Unlike a computer, which can fail in seemingly count-less and creative ways, the traditional iPod exhibits only a few behaviors when it's feeling poorly. Following are the most common problems and (when available) their solutions.

The missing iPod

When you plug your iPod into your Mac or PC, it should make its presence known in short order, appearing in iTunes. If you've configured your iPod to mount as a disk drive, it will also materialize and remain on the Mac's Desktop or within Windows' My Computer window.

If your Macintosh-formatted iPod refuses to mount, restart your Mac while holding down the Shift key. This boots Macs running Mac OS X into Safe Mode. iPods that do not mount otherwise have been known to do so on Macs running in Safe Mode.

If that doesn't do the trick—or if this trick isn't appli-cable because you're using your iPod with a Windows PC—first reset the iPod. For an iPod shuffle, this entails simply switching the iPod off for 5 seconds. For a click-wheel iPod, hold down both the Center and Menu buttons for 6 seconds. For a 1G, 2G, or 3G iPod, plug it into a power outlet, and hold down the Play and Menu buttons for 6 seconds.

If your nonshuffle traditional iPod still won't mount, try forcing it into Disk Mode, as follows: Repeat the reset procedure described above, and when you see the Apple logo on the iPod screen, hold down the Center and Play buttons (click-wheel iPods) or the Previous and Next buttons (1G, 2G, and 3G iPods).

Obviously, none of these techniques is a good long-term solution, as you don't want to restart your Mac in Safe Mode, reset the iPod, or force it into Disk Mode whenever you sync it. An iPod that won't mount is one that should be restored with the latest iPod software, which is accessible through the iPod's Summary tab in iTunes.

PC laptops may not recognize a connected iPod if the computer is configured to turn off power to the USB ports to conserve power. To prevent this from happening, choose Start > Control Panel, double-click the System icon, click the Hardware tab, and click the Device Manager button. In the resulting window, locate the Universal Serial Bus entry in the list of devices, and click the plus sign (+) next to the entry to expand it. Double-click each USB Root Hub entry, click the Power Management tab (*phew, almost finished...*), disable the Allow the Computer to Turn off This Device to Save Power option, click OK to dismiss the window, and restart the computer.

The confused iPod

Clues that your iPod is confused include the absence of videos, playlists, artists, and songs that used to be there; the failure of the iPod to boot beyond the Apple logo; and the appearance of a folder icon with an exclamation point. In the following sections, I look at these scenarios (which don't apply to the iPod shuffle because it isn't complex enough to get confused in these ways).

Absence of items

While I was attempting to use a Macintosh-formatted traditional iPod on a Windows PC, my PC crashed, and when I unplugged the iPod, its playlists were missing. I could still play music from the iPod through the Songs screen, but things were not right.

In an attempt to restore a sense of sanity to my iPod, I tried these remedies:

1. Reset the iPod (again, for click-wheel iPods, press and hold Select and Menu for 6 seconds; for 1G, 2G, and 3G iPods, plug into a power source and then press and hold Play and Menu for 6 seconds).

   Resetting the iPod is similar to pushing the Reset switch on your computer; it forces the iPod to restart and (ideally) get its little house in order. In this case, the iPod remained confused.

2. Restore the iPod.

   If resetting doesn't work, or if your iPod can't seem to find its operating system (it displays a folder icon with an exclamation point), there's nothing else for it than to restore the iPod to its original factory state—meaning that all the data on it is removed, and the iPod's firmware is updated.

To restore the iPod with iTunes 7 or later, just plug the iPod into your computer's powered USB port (or FireWire port, for older iPods), and click the iPod's icon in the iTunes Source list. In the Summary tab, you'll see an option to restore the iPod (**Figure 9.1**). Click the Restore button. The iPod will be reformatted and,

with just a little luck, will perform in a more acceptable manner.

Figure 9.1
The Restore
button, located
in the Summary
tab of the iPod
panel.

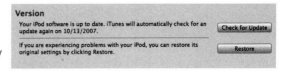

Version

Your iPod software is up to date. iTunes will automatically check for an update again on 10/13/2007.   Check for Update

If you are experiencing problems with your iPod, you can restore its original settings by clicking Restore.   Restore

To put your songs back on the iPod, just sync the iPod
with iTunes in your preferred manner.

note

On very rare occasions, restoring the iPod on a computer
platform other than the one you usually use can make
the iPod more cooperative. In other words, if restoring the
iPod on a Macintosh doesn't work, try restoring it on a
Windows PC (or vice versa).

Failure to boot

There are a few possible reasons why an iPod may
not boot beyond the Apple logo, some benign, and
others not so:

The Hold switch is on. Go ahead and smack yourself
in the head (and then breathe a sigh of relief) if
your iPod won't start up because the Hold switch
is engaged.

Drained battery. Among the most benign problems
is an iPod battery that's drained (though not dead;
I discuss dead iPod batteries in the "Assault on
Batteries" sidebar later in this chapter). If the iPod
is functioning normally otherwise, switching it on
when its battery is very nearly drained causes a low-
battery icon to appear on the display. If the battery

is completely drained, the iPod can't even muster the energy to display this icon; the screen remains black, and the drive refuses to spin up. Plug your iPod into the power adapter or your computer, and let it charge. If everything's hunky-dory after that, pat yourself on the back for a job well done.

If you've plugged the iPod's data/power cable into a computer that isn't currently charging it—one that's turned off or asleep, for example—unplug the iPod. Some people have reported that when the iPod is plugged in but isn't being charged, its power can dissipate quickly.

If your computer won't charge your iPod, it's possible that something is wrong with its USB or FireWire port. Try plugging your iPod into a different port or power adapter. If the iPod charges, it's time to cock a suspicious eyebrow at your computer.

In some rare cases, the battery may not be charged enough for the iPod to be reset. If you've tried other solutions and failed, unplug the iPod from a power supply for 24 hours; then plug it into a power source and attempt to reset it.

Songs skip

Songs played on the iPod may skip for several reasons, which include:

Large song files. Large song files (long symphonic movements or those endless Grateful Dead jams, for example) don't play particularly well with the 32 MB RAM buffer on some iPods with hard drives. (Recent high-capacity iPods have a larger RAM buffer and do better with long files.) Large song files race through the RAM buffer, requiring the iPod to access the hard drive more often. This situation can lead to skipping if the iPod is pulling the song almost directly from the hard drive. If possible, reduce the sizes of files by employing greater compression, or chop really long files (such as audiobooks) into pieces.

Damaged file. A damaged song file may skip. If you find that the same song skips every time you play it—and other songs seem to play back with no problem—go back to the source of the song (an audio CD, for example), rip the song again, and replace the copy on the iPod with the newly ripped version.

iPod that needs to be reset. Yes, an iPod that needs to be reset may cause songs to skip. (Refer to "The confused iPod" earlier in this chapter for instructions.)

iPod that needs to be restored. If a reset won't do the trick, make sure that all the data on your iPod is backed up, and restore the iPod from the iPod panel's Summary tab. (Instructions for doing so are in "The confused iPod" earlier in this chapter.)

Unpleasant sound as the hard drive spins up

This symptom appeared in some early releases of the 4G iPods and a very few color iPods. Typically, iPods with this problem will make noise through the Headphone port whenever the hard drive spins up. Static accompanies the first couple of seconds of songs played after the iPod spins up.

This problem appears to be a grounding issue that makes itself known only when you've plugged in headphones whose audio connector bears a metal base that comes into contact with the iPod's case. This metal-to-metal contact transmits this sound through your headphones. To troubleshoot the issue, place a small plastic washer on the post of any affected headphones.

The really confused iPod

Your iPod may be so confused that it won't mount on your Mac's Desktop or in Windows' My Computer window and can't be restored. Follow these steps to mount the iPod:

1. Connect a 1G, 2G, or 3G iPod to a built-in FireWire port on your computer (rather than an unpowered FireWire port on a PC Card or a USB 2.0 port, for example).

   Because the click-wheel iPods can be powered via a USB 2.0 connection, feel free to use such a connection with your Mac or Windows PC.

2. Reset the 1G, 2G, or 3G iPod by holding down the Play and Menu buttons for 6 seconds. Reset the click-wheel iPods by holding down Select and Menu for 6 seconds.

3. When you see the Apple logo, hold down the Previous and Next buttons on the first three generations of the iPod until you see a message that reads "Do not disconnect." On the click-wheel iPods, hold down Select and Play.

The key combination outlined in step 2 resets the iPod much like pressing the Reset switch on a PC or Mac resets the computer. The second key combination forces the iPod into Disk Mode—a mode that will help your computer recognize and mount the iPod.

With luck, your iPod should appear on the Mac's Desktop or in Windows' My Computer window. Then you should be able to restore it.

Secret Button Combinations

By pressing the proper combination of buttons on the iPod's face, you can force the device to reset, enter Disk Mode, and scan its hard disk for damage. Here are those combinations and the wonders they perform:

RESET

When you reset your iPod, your data remains intact, but the iPod restores the factory settings. This technique reboots the iPod and is helpful when your iPod is locked up.

Click-wheel iPods: Plug the iPod into a powered device (the Apple iPod Power Adapter, an auto adapter, or a built-in FireWire port) or a high-powered USB 2.0 port; then hold down the Center and Menu buttons for 6 seconds.

iPod shuffle: Disconnect the shuffle from your computer, move the power switch to the Off position, wait 5 seconds, and switch it back to On (or to the Play in Order or Shuffle position for the 1G iPod shuffle). (Yes, resetting a shuffle is really nothing more than turning it off and on again.)

continues on next page

Secret Button Combinations *continued*

First three generations of the full-size iPod: Plug the iPod into a powered FireWire device (the Apple iPod Power Adapter, an auto adapter, or a built-in FireWire port), and hold down Play and Menu for 6 seconds.

DISK SCAN

Use this method to check the integrity of an older iPod's hard drive. This test can take 15 to 20 minutes, so be patient. Be sure to plug your iPod into the power adapter when you perform this test so that the iPod doesn't run out of juice before the scan is complete. If the scan shows no problems, a check mark appears over the disk icon on the first three generations of the full-size iPod.

First three generations of the full-size iPod: Reset the iPod. At the Apple logo, hold down the Previous, Next, Center, and Menu buttons. An animated icon of a disc and magnifying glass with a progress bar below it appears.

Click-wheel iPods: These iPods don't offer a button combination to scan the hard drive.

DISK MODE

Use this technique when you need to mount your iPod on a Mac with an unpowered FireWire card (a FireWire PC Card in your older PowerBook, for example) or on a PC with a similarly unpowered FireWire or USB 2.0 connection.

Click-wheel iPods: Reset the iPod. When the Apple logo appears, hold down the Center and Play buttons. (On more recent iPods, you may have better luck pressing Center and Play after the iPod resets but before you see the Apple logo.)

First three generations of the full-size iPod: Reset the iPod. When you see the Apple logo, hold down the Previous and Next buttons.

The frozen iPod

Just like a computer, the iPod can freeze from time to time. To thaw it, attach your iPod to a power source—the power adapter, a powered FireWire port, or a computer's high-powered USB 2.0 port—and, on the first three generations of the iPod, hold down the Play and Menu buttons for 6 seconds. For click-wheel iPods, hold down the Center and Menu buttons for the same 6 seconds.

Failure to charge

An iPod might not charge for several reasons, including all of the following:

A sleeping computer. The iPod may not charge when it's attached to a sleeping computer. (Some sleeping computers will charge an iPod; others won't.) If you suspect that a sleepy computer is the problem, wake up your computer if you want the iPod to charge.

The wrong cable. Remember, a USB 2.0 connection carries no power to 3G iPods (though it does to click-wheel iPods). To charge your 1G, 2G, or 3G iPod on a Windows PC, you must plug your iPod into a powered FireWire port or the iPod's power adapter.

More than one FireWire device on the chain. Although you can chain multiple FireWire devices, doing so with an iPod isn't such a good idea. To begin with, a FireWire device on the chain before the iPod (a hard drive, for example) may be hogging all the power. Second, there have been reports of iPods that got corrupted when they were left on a chain with other FireWire devices. To be safe rather than sorry, don't put the iPod on a FireWire chain. If you must use multiple FireWire devices, purchase a powered FireWire hub (which costs between $45 and $65).

A frozen iPod. An iPod that's frozen won't charge. Reset the iPod with the instructions given in "The confused iPod" earlier in the chapter.

A faulty cable. Cables break. Try a different data/power cable, just in case yours has gone the way of the dodo.

A faulty computer port. It's possible that the FireWire or USB 2.0 port on your computer has given up the ghost. If you have one, try charging the iPod from an Apple iPod Power Adapter.

A funky power adapter. The Apple iPod Power Adapter could also be bad. Attempt to charge your iPod from your computer.

A faulty data/power port on the iPod. This problem is more common on 1G and 2G iPods than it is on later iPods. As you plug and unplug the FireWire cable from the iPod's FireWire port on these old iPods, it's possible to put too much stress on the internal connectors that deliver power to your iPod's FireWire port, breaking the bond between those connectors and your iPod's motherboard.

A dead battery. Like all lithium-ion batteries, the iPod's battery is good for 400 to 500 full charges. When you've exhausted those charges, your iPod needs a new battery. See the sidebar "Assault on Batteries" for more details.

Broken iPod. iPods occasionally break. If none of these solutions brings your iPod back from its never-ending slumber, it may need to be replaced. Contact Apple at http://depot.info.apple.com/ipod.

Assault on Batteries

There's been a great deal of hoopla surrounding the iPod's battery—specifically, how long it should last and why it's so darned difficult to replace. Let me set the record straight.

Nearly all iPods carry a lithium-ion (Li-ion) battery. (The iPod touch has a lithium-polymer battery, just as the iPhone does.) Theoretically, Li-ion batteries, by their very nature, can be fully charged up to 500 times. In actual practice, your iPod's battery will put up with between 300 and 450 complete charges before it gives up the ghost.

This is all well and good if you charge your iPod once a week or so. But if you use your iPod constantly—and, thus, fully charge it four or five times a week—you'll discover that after about a year and a half, it's kaput.

As you might imagine, those who've seen their iPods kick the bucket after a year and a half have been less than joyous about it. After all, a device you paid several hundred dollars for should have a longer shelf life than a Twinkie. Adding to this unhappiness was Apple's policy of charging $255 to replace the iPod.

Apple and some third-party battery vendors got hip to the situation as the first couple of revisions of the iPod began to go south due to dead batteries.

continues on next page

Assault on Batteries, *continued*

If your iPod is more than a year old, and it fails to hold a charge, Apple will replace it with another "functionally equivalent new, used, or refurbished iPod" for $59 (plus $6.95 for shipping). That "functionally equivalent" stuff means that you won't get back the same iPod that you send in. You'll get one from the "good pile" that has the same capacity and is of the same generation as the one you sent in. If you send in an engraved iPod, Apple will take the back plate off your iPod and put it on the replacement iPod. For more details, visit http://depot.info.apple.com/ipod.

If you're mechanically inclined, it's fairly easy to replace the battery in a 1G or 2G iPod. A Google search will turn up any number of companies willing to sell you a replacement iPod battery, plus the tools and instructions necessary to open the iPod. But newer models are tougher nuts to crack. The iPod mini is particularly difficult to open, for example. And the 3G iPod includes a thin cable that's attached to both the motherboard and a connector on the back plate; open it the wrong way, and you could break the cable, destroying your iPod.

For this reason, it's safest to have a professional install your new battery. iResQ (www.iresq.com) offers a battery-replacement service for $54, and Other World Computing (http://eshop.macsales.com) will install a Newer Technology NuPower battery for the price of the part plus a $39 service charge.

The broken iPod

It's a machine, and regrettably, machines break. If none of these solutions brings your iPod back from the dead, it may need to be repaired. If you live near an Apple Store or another outfit that sells iPods, take it in. If such a trip is impractical, contact Apple at http://depot.info.apple.com/ipod for instructions on how to have your iPod serviced.

When you take a misbehaving iPod to a Genius at the Apple Store, said Genius will run a couple of tests on it. If it fails to respond, the Genius may try to restore it (which is why you should always have a backup of your music and data).

If that doesn't work, and your iPod is under warranty, you'll probably get a replacement on the spot (provided that Apple still sells the same iPod model, with the same storage capacity, as the one you bring in). If Apple's changed the iPod line—you've got a 80 GB 5G iPod, for example, and Apple sells 80 and 160 GB iPod classics—according to Apple, your iPod "will be replaced with functionally equivalent new, used, or refurbished iPod equipment." In other words, you're unlikely to get the next size up, even though it sells for the same price you originally paid for yours. If the iPod is out of warranty, you'll have to pay for the repair.

Troubleshooting the iPod touch

The iPod touch may be an engineering marvel, but even engineering marvels get moody from time to time. And when your iPod misbehaves, you're bound to be in a hurry to put things right. Allow me to lend a hand by suggesting the following troubleshooting techniques.

The basics

If your iPod touch acts up in a general way—won't turn on, won't appear in iTunes, or quits and locks up—try these techniques.

No iPod startup

Is your iPod just sitting there, with its cold black screen mocking you? If you have an iPod charger lying around the house, try using it rather than a USB 2.0 port. If you get no response after about 10 minutes, try another electrical outlet. Still nothing? Try a different iPod cable.

Still no go, even though you've had that iPod for a long time and use it constantly? The battery may be dead (but this shouldn't happen in your first year of ownership, regardless of how much you use it).

No iPod in iTunes

If your iPod doesn't appear in iTunes when you connect it to your computer, try these steps:

1. Make sure your iPod is charged.

   If the battery is completely dead, it may need about 10 minutes of charging before it can be roused enough to make an iTunes appearance.

2. Be sure the iPod is plugged into a USB 2.0 port.

   Your computer won't recognize the iPod touch when it's attached to a USB 1.0 port.

3. Plug your iPod into a different USB 2.0 port.

4. Unplug the iPod, turn it off and then on, and plug it back in.

5. Use a different iPod cable (if you have one).

6. Restart your computer, and try again.

7. Reinstall iTunes.

The Four Rs

In this section, I refer to four troubleshooting techniques: resign, restart, reset, and restore. In order of seriousness (and desirability), they are:

- **Resign.** Force-quit the current application by holding down the Home button for about 6 seconds. This step should get you out of a frozen application and return you to the iPod's Home screen.

- **Restart.** Turn the iPod off and then on. Hold down the Sleep/Wake button until a red slider appears that reads *Slide to Power Off*. Slide the slider, and the iPod shuts off. Now press the Sleep/Wake button to turn on the iPod.

- **Reset.** Press and hold the Home and Sleep/Wake buttons for about 10 seconds—until the Apple logo appears—and then let go. This step is akin to resetting your computer by holding down its power switch until it's forced to reboot.

- **Restore.** Plug your iPod into your computer, launch iTunes, select the iPod in iTunes' Source list, click the Summary tab, and click the Restore button. This step wipes out all the data on your iPod and installs a clean version of its operating system.

Unresponsive (and uncooperative) applications

Just like the programs running on your computer, your iPod's applications can act up, freezing or quitting unexpectedly. You can try a few things to nudge your iPod into action. If the first step doesn't work, march to the next:

1. Resign from the application.

   If an application refused to do anything, it's likely frozen. The only way to thaw it is to force it to quit. Press and hold the Home button until you return to the Home screen.

2. Clear Safari's cache.

   If you find that Safari quits suddenly, something in its cache may be corrupted, and clearing the cache may solve the problem. To do so, tap Settings in the Home screen; then tap Safari, and in the Safari Settings screen, tap Clear Cache.

3. Reset the iPod by holding down the Home and Sleep/Wake buttons until you see the Apple logo.

4. On the iPod, go to the General setting; tap Reset and then tap Reset All Settings.

   This step resets the iPod's preferences but doesn't delete any of your data or media.

5. In that same Reset screen, tap Erase All Content and Settings (**Figure 9.2**).

Figure 9.2
Erasing all the content and settings from your iPod is the next-to-last resort.

 This step vaporizes not only the iPod's preferences, but its media content as well. Before doing this, try to sync your iPod so that you can save any contacts and bookmarks you've created.

6. Restore the iPod.

Sunk by sync

Data should move smoothly between your computer and your iPod, but it doesn't always. Try these fixes.

iPod runs out of free space

You may see an error message indicating that the iPod doesn't have enough free space to sync all the data and media you've selected in iTunes. If you inadvertently unplugged the iPod during a sync, some data may be left on it, taking up space. To remove this excess data, disable music and photo syncing in iTunes, and click the Apply button to sync the iPod. This step should erase the data. Now enable music and photo syncing, and click Apply again to sync your media.

Another possibility is that you're simply asking the iPod to suck up too much media. You may have accumulated a lot of video podcasts since your last sync, for example, and the iPod just doesn't have room for all of them. Try disabling files that take up a lot of storage—TV shows, movies, and video podcasts—and then sync the iPod. Look at the Capacity bar to see how much space remains, and choose media based on that remaining space.

Yahoo Address Book won't sync

If you receive an exception error when attempting to sync Yahoo Address Book contacts, one of the contacts in your regular address book may have an ill-formatted address. If you have *billybob.example. com* instead of *billybob@example.com*, you may see this error. Check the addresses in the program that holds the contacts you sync with your iPod.

Index